THEY DARED TO
MAKE A DIFFERENCE

Printed in Wales by Cambrian Printers, Aberystwyth

THEY DARED TO
MAKE A DIFFERENCE

The story of three generations of women
behind Rachel's Dairy

by
Teleri Bevan

FOREWORD

by

Sir Meuric Rees

The history of three generations of the Brynllys family in Ceredigion has been a voyage of discovery for the author Teleri Bevan and will be a source of inspiration to everyone who reads it.

There are two traits that are common to all pioneers – vision and determination. These shine through the lives of Bessie, Dinah and Rachel, and from my own association with them, I know that these traits have been enhanced by an innate measure of common sense, courtesy and consideration for others.

I well remember visiting Brynllys Farm on an Open Day and wondering whether the emphasis on self-sufficiency and a quality product would be sustainable when the current indication was to increase output to cover rising costs. It needed courage to maintain the concept and for Brynllys to become the first certified organic dairy farm in the United Kingdom. Today organic food products indicate a certain natural quality and are at a premium.

It is remarkable that a heavy snowstorm in 1982 has led to the present Rachel's Dairy, trading internationally from the Glanyrafon Industrial Estate at Aberystwyth. It is a story of success in business, richly interlaced with the humanity and personal aspects of family life in a farming community.

I feel privileged to contribute this foreword and would suggest that the three principals have been blessed with compatible partners. Life is so much more fulfilled if the highs and lows can be shared. I know that Gareth, a Tywyn boy, was a tower of strength to the family in the risk taking days of the rapid expansion of the modern premises.

As I turned to the last page of the story, I was reminded of an apposite quotation that I heard many years ago:

'Work without vision is drudgery
Vision without work is but a dream
Put the two together and anything can be achieved.'

I know of no better example than this saga of a unique family.

INTRODUCTION

This is a story which spans a century of endeavour, determination and conviction by three generations of farming women - Bessie Brown, Dinah Jones and Rachel Rowlands.

Today Rachel's Dairy is a global company, its milk products of yogurt, cream, and butter produced in Wales are internationally recognised on supermarket shelves around the world. Each generation has made a distinctive contribution to the growth of the organic system of farming, and writing of their experiences has for me, been a journey down the lane of childhood memories.

I had no idea of the connection between my family and Bessie or Mrs Jones as I remember her – the tall, distinguished farmer of Nantllan and Glanymor in the Clarach Valley just north of Aberystwyth. During those pre-war years we were neighbours and as my research gathered pace, this became a personal journey of discovery and I too have been enriched, as I hope readers will be, not only by three lives of courage, dedication and achievement, but also by familial loyalty, great joy and the sadness of loss.

The story begins in 1879 when Bessie Brown was born on a tenant farm on one of the largest estates in Scotland...

Teleri Bevan

ELIZABETH
(Bessie)

ELIZABETH
(Bessie)

Bessie Brown was different, even at birth. There was a pronounced air of strength and nobility about her and, as she grew up on a large estate in the heart of the Angus glens, the influence of nature and nurture, in equal measure, moulded her character. She was born in Scotland, four miles from Glamis Castle, the fairy-tale fortress dominating the landscape of the Strathmore Valley with its high slender towers, turrets, spires and the soft pink tones of the solid stone walls.

As a strategic stronghold it had a long history dating from 1372, when it was presented by Robert the Bruce to Sir John Lyon, for services to his country, a man of surpassing ability, noble talent and great charm of person and manner, known as the 'Whyte Lyon' because of his fair complexion. His descendants, through marriage, became Bowes Lyon and the Earls of Strathmore, but ghosts from past centuries have added colour to the bare bones of history.

A grey lady prays in the castle's chapel; another woman without a tongue parades the grounds; a nobleman, Alexander, Earl of Crawford is said to be gambling with the devil in a secret room; and a young black boy, a negro servant, haunts the stone seat outside the Queen's bedroom. It is also the setting for Shakespeare's tragedy Macbeth, and among the most haunting parts of the castle is Duncan's Hall, which commemorates the slaying of King Duncan by Macbeth, although the actual killing took place near Elgin. The story of Glamis Castle as portrayed in the play, although historically incorrect, remains the traditional Shakespeare scene of the crime.

Its colourful history, coupled with the plethora of apparitions who appear within the walls from time to time, may account for the number of people who visit the castle every year. However it is more likely they have also come to see the birthplace and ancestral home of Elizabeth Bowes Lyon, Queen Elizabeth, the Queen Mother (1900-2002).

Bessie Brown, or, to be correct, Elizabeth Lyon Brown, was born in 1879 to William and Helen Brown, tenant farmers on the Glamis Estate. The Lyon name represents valour and strength originating in France as 'de Leonne' and several strands of the present day Lyon surname occur in and around the glens and valleys of the Strathmore Estate.

The Lyon in Bessie's name was inherited from her mother Helen, who, like her future husband William, was born and brought up on the estate. Her father, Joseph Lyon was a farmer and by dint of hard work made his tenancy one of the most productive and prosperous in the area, where he was admired for his farming know-how and knowledge. He built walls to enclose fields and control his livestock and, to manage his grassland, he would travel to Dundee to collect animal bones from slaughter houses, grind them into powder to spread as fertiliser on the land. The rent at that time was £3 an acre and it remained so throughout his farming years, despite asking every year for it to be reduced. He lived until he was 89 years old and his granddaughter, Bessie, spent a great deal of time in his company in her early teenage years listening to his stories and learning about farming systems and practices.

Helen, his daughter, had had little interest in farming and worked as a school teacher in Manchester before she married William and they settled as tenant farmers at Lower Drumgley, a farm of 200 acres some four miles from Glamis Castle.

The tenancy had been in William's family for many years, but it had been a rough tract of stony land until William's father turned it into a fruitful enterprise for rearing sheep and cattle. The solid stone house had been built by the Earl from material hewn from one of the estate's quarries, as had other farm buildings including barns, sheds and a cowshed. It was the tenant's responsibility to care for livestock and land, to build walls around fields and keep them in good repair. The family believed their graft and persistence would bring stability and permanence to their lives on an estate which, when Bessie was born, had expanded to 22,000 acres.

Her parents were proud people who worked hard to make a living. Bessie inherited from them those qualities that matter most and included many influences which profoundly guided the course of her life. It was a life of service to her family and to agriculture, which began on a tenant farm in Scotland and ended as a successful landowner on the shores of Cardigan Bay in West Wales. In many respects she was before her time, and yet Bessie was also a woman of her time. A learning process which began with the rigours of life in a remote rural environment taught her how to observe and care, to notice the signs heralding the rhythm of the seasons, to understand the effect of weather on land and soil, to respect the natural needs of animals and crops and to be diligent at work and considerate of others.

In the years before Bessie was born there had been considerable unrest and strife in the Highlands and Islands of Scotland between landowners, crofters and tenants, at a time of greed and callousness. Crofters were evicted, dispossessed, uprooted and re-located because landowners had realised that planting large tracts of deer forests and increasing their sheep flocks would be much more profitable than having to rely on the income they received from crofters' tenancies. There was violence, agitation and bloodshed as crofters demanded a review and reform of their rights and the year after Bessie was born, 1880, a commission was established. Six years later a government act ensured that all crofters and tenants in Scotland had security of tenure and fair rents. The 'Highland Clearances', as the despised practice became known, had denuded the area of its people and its spirit but it also ensured that tenant farmers in Scotland had, at last, a measure of security.

Unlike many landowners of the north, the thirteenth Earl of Strathmore was seen as a considerate and generous landlord and William and Helen avoided the turmoil experienced by crofters. Theirs were the low lying lands in a productive grassy valley near the Loch of Forfar and the surrounding hillsides were heather covered moorland, upland grazing or forestry plantations. The main industry, apart from agriculture, was the linen trade. The mill on the estate, the most advanced in terms of machinery and power, employed over 60 men to spin flax grown locally and in the late 19th century over 4000 pieces of brown linen were manufactured annually, chiefly for Dundee markets.

The Earl was much respected by his tenants for his deep knowledge of farming practices and as a breeder of prize-winning animals of quality - polled cattle, Clydesdale horses and Shropshire sheep. The Glamis Estate became renowned as a cattle breeding centre and tenant farmers found ready markets at local fairs where prime cattle were bought and sent to Dundee to be sold to other parts of the country. The Earl spent large sums of money on remodelling many farm buildings, fencing and road building, and during the great cattle plague caused by the disease Rinderpest - an infectious and fatal viral disease of cattle - he bore with his tenants the heavy financial loss estimated at that time to be in the region of £24,000.

Most of the Lower Drumgley farm inherited from William's father was now of good quality land and although they lived a frugal life, without fripperies, it was comfortable and solid. It was against this thrifty and testing background that Bessie, the second of six, three brothers and three sisters, grew up. They were well educated at the local junior and grammar schools in Forfar. Education to improve the family situation was deeply felt by both parents but Bessie was the only one of the six children to pursue a course of further education. The boys went into farming and Dave the eldest, as was the custom, inherited his father's tenancy. The other two boys accepted other tenancies on the estate, but William, their father, was much more interested in mending and designing machinery, becoming an engineer, a strong family attribute passed on from generation to generation. The youngest daughter, Jennie, referred to by the next generation of the family as Aunty Jen, stayed at home to look after her parents, the fate of so many last born daughters of large families.

Bessie was tough, determined and ambitious and as she grew up, she controlled her exuberance and channelled her ambitions. She was clever and bright and had come to realise that education was the route to freedom of choice. She knew from her early years that aspects of agriculture would feature in her further education. Without doubt Bessie would have liked to farm but, as a woman, obtaining a tenancy would be virtually impossible. She had a close relationship with her father and his influence had a lasting effect but Bessie always knew that the tenancy of their farm would be handed to Dave, the eldest son.

She completed her studies at school with flying colours and was accepted to study agriculture at Glasgow University under Sir Robert Patrick Wright, a leading academic who was in the process of compiling twelve volumes of *The Standard Encyclopedia of Modern Agriculture and Rural Economy*, published eventually in 1911. Bessie followed a basic two year course in agriculture studying farming systems and animal husbandry and her intention was to take a further two year course in dairying in order to qualify for the National Diploma in Dairying (NDD). Sir Robert claimed that she was one of the brightest students he had ever taught and gave her a glowing recommendation to follow her second course at the University of Reading.

It was a bold step, but dairying was growing in importance and universities at the turn of the century were expanding, in particular

17

at Reading. The Department of Agriculture had been established in 1893 when the British Dairy Institute was transferred to the site and 65 students enrolled in the first year. Dairying appealed to women. Girls and farmers wives were often portrayed as milkmaids, always looking happy, skipping along carrying their three legged stools and pails of milk, feeding calves, milking cows and making butter. In reality though it was a tough life, milking cows by hand twice a day in all weathers, summer and winter, carrying hay and feed from barns to cowsheds and the daily drudge of cleaning, brushing and carrying water in order to keep cows and cowsheds clean and free of disease.

When Bessie joined the vocational course at Reading in 1897, there was great emphasis and importance on the practical aspects of dairying as a subject. The infectious disease, tuberculosis (TB), known as 'consumption' was spreading. Research had also proved that there was a correlation between TB in cattle and humans. There was no absolute cure but improving public health care, better diets and clean social and sanitary conditions strengthened the body's defences against the disease. Farmers were being encouraged to produce cleaner and better quality milk products and to monitor their cattle regularly for tell-tale signs of the disease.

The two years at Reading proved to be a life-changing experience. Bessie worked hard and played hard. The course was a satisfying mix of classroom lectures and practical experience on farms and dairies. It included the principles of producing good quality milk, identifying the characteristics of productive dairy cows, housing and feeding, breeding and the essence of making milk products such as butter, cheese and yogurt to a high standard. She made the most of the experience, maturing, making friends - men and women - and absorbing different views and attitudes without necessarily agreeing with them. She was always forthright in discussion, never afraid to voice her opinions although she maintained she was not an academic. But there was only one drawback. Reading was a very long way from home and Bessie often complained of the long journey at the beginning and end of every term.

The Browns were a close-knit family and her parents could see she was thriving although one of her siblings once said of her, "Bessie won't get on, she won't get anywhere. She's got no chin." It was some years later when Bessie had achieved a measure of success, that she found an adequate riposte, "Well, I've done everything, despite my chin!"

She was not glamorous, not all that interested in clothes and fashion, there being anyway little money, but everyone who met her realised she was a person of determination and distinction coupled with a wicked sense of humour. Her face was open and friendly, clear skinned and fair haired and often smiling in repose, a sign of an out-going personality and a veracious one. There were other times when she could be forthright and fiery in argument to show her displeasure. She was tall, her carriage and demeanour the obvious outward sign of strength of character.

During all her years of studies, Bessie relied heavily on her experiences at Lower Drumgley and she remembered the systems farmers followed in the Angus glens. They rarely used chemical fertilisers, weed killers or pesticides; they practised traditional ways and she often recalled her father's wise teachings. He called their traditional system, 'natural farming' as did her grandfather, Joseph Lyon. It was a philosophy and practice that was deeply ingrained and one that Bessie was to pursue throughout her life. Historically Glamis had been a prosperous production and trading centre but the approach of the new century brought times of transition. Mechanisation was increasing, power from steam and electricity had transformed local industries, including agriculture, and the need for manual labour was decreasing. Many were attracted to the industrial areas of heavy industry, coal mining and ship building. Others were enticed by the stories of land and wealth in the new world of the United States, Canada and Britain's other colonies. It was a time when depopulation from the countryside gathered pace. Bessie also realised that a tenant who had not long obtained security of tenure by law still remained dependent on the patronage of the laird for the right to farm.

Half the private land in Scotland was owned by a mere 100 landowners and as the century drew to a close, it became apparent that landowners were looking for new profitable enterprises. Slowly the emphasis of land management changed. Sport and country pursuits took over from sheep; valuable grassland kept for grazing cattle became moorland for grouse shooting and forests became breeding grounds for deer stalking. But it was sport for the privileged few.

At Reading Bessie was aware of all these changes in land management. She achieved her NDD qualification with ease and her first job took her back to Scotland, an opportunity to live and work not too far from the Glamis Estate. There was reform and change in agricultural education too. The University of Glasgow amalgamated its own Agricultural Department with the Scottish Dairy Institute and the West of Scotland Technical College to form one campus, the West of Scotland Agricultural College based at Auchincruive. Bessie had been earmarked by her first mentor, Sir Robert Wright for a post at the college and he persuaded her to return to be a Dairy Instructress. Bessie was 20 years old and looked set for a career in the foothills of the Grampians.

However, within just a few weeks, the relationship between her and the manager of the dairy became difficult and the fiery and forthright side of her character surfaced. Bessie quickly realised she could never persuade him to agree to her ideas, and he, in all probability, felt that she was headstrong and far too young. Bessie packed her bags and returned south to manage a large dairy near Oxford where she gained more practical experience and formed other friendships.

In due course, as the new century dawned and family celebrations were in full swing, Bessie's life took another turn. An opportunity beckoned which was to change her life irrevocably. In October 1900, Bessie Brown went to Wales.

*　　*　　*　　*　　*

Bessie arrived on a golden Autumn day to begin a new life in a new century at a new academic establishment. She had been appointed as the very first Dairy Instructor under the aegis of the Agricultural Department at the University College of Wales, Aberystwyth. There had been more than enough time during the long train journey from Scotland to reflect on the wisdom of the panel who appointed her at such a young age. She was 21, with little work or teaching experience, but there were glowing recommendations from her referees in Reading and Scotland. They knew Bessie was resolute and tough, two characteristics of a Scot who could claim to be a descendant of the Picts and Celts, traditionally known as colourful and excitable people and always prepared to attack problems head on.

She had also realised, and felt it to the end of her days, that her appointment to this Welsh academic institution in far West Wales was due to her Celtic inheritance as she was the only candidate who was not English. The post carried twin objectives; to set up dairy teaching courses for students and to advise the conservative-minded local farmers on the principles of agricultural science.

The College was comparatively new, having opened its doors in 1872 with few departments and 26 students. Lack of finance delayed the establishment of a Department of Agriculture for 20 years but the College believed firmly that it had an obligation to assist the main industry of the area. However there were rumblings and objections when the formal proposal to set up a course in dairying was mooted. Many felt that technical instruction in butter and cheese-making bore little relation to genuine university course work. Yet Bessie had been trained at two universities who had pioneered the merits of the subject by merging the Dairy Institute in Scotland with University of Glasgow, and the British Dairy Institute with the University of Reading. No such institutions had been established in Wales and the decision for the expansion at Aberystwyth to establish community short courses was deemed vital if the College was to maintain the goodwill of county councils and crucially, to receive financial backing from them.

The College's dairy was an unprepossessing space in the cellar next to the men's cloakroom of the Old College building by the sea. There, Bessie and her assistant Miss Rutherford battled against noise and fought for cleaner conditions and better hygiene. Worse, when she and the assistant were churning butter or attempting to get milk to curdle at the correct and constant temperature, the coal central heating boiler - also in the basement - had to be discontinued. The Principal recorded the dilemma in a note, 'If we keep students warm in a cold April and May, we melt the cheeses!'

Bessie was made of stern stuff and was determined not to allow such matters to interfere with her goal. She campaigned for better resources but she also set up lectures for College students, expanded the courses and slowly began to establish practical instruction in farmhouses and village halls as part her extra-mural work.

Professor Tom Parry who led the department in 1896 had already been holding classes and had found increasing interest from many sections of the community. Over 40 women attended a six week instruction course in the Church Hall in the parish of Llangwyryfon where Miss Rutherford had managed to transport and place four big butter churns. Every participant was invited to bring their own cream. They were then divided into groups and given guidance and instruction in cleanliness, temperatures and procedures necessary to make quality butter. After completing the course, they were awarded a certificate which, for those interested, enabled them to attend a further course at University College, Aberystwyth as part-time students.

Bessie found this kind of work appealing. She was meeting different people, guiding them with their problems and giving demonstrations. She found startling contrasts between Scotland and Wales. Traditionally the Welsh cowshed and dairy practice was very basic with little concern for hygiene, rarely using hot water to wash the pans and bowls when they had finished butter making.

The Department of Agriculture was rapidly expanding, but it lacked leadership and cohesion, and there was much academic bickering. A new Professor and Director was appointed, Bryner Jones, and he soon reorganised the department. The number of lectureships was reduced and he succeeded in galvanising and enthusing the remaining staff to give them clarity of purpose. The dairying section had his full backing and he hoped finance would be forthcoming to build a new purposefully designed building. However, it took at least another 20 years to realise the dream. Meanwhile, the extra-mural community work was continuing strongly and Bessie travelled to remote farmsteads in Mid Wales by train, bus and bike, showing true stamina.

One of her early visits took her on a journey of about 40 miles north to an isolated farm in Llanbrynmair and the experience seemed to epitomise all the old ways, superstition and beliefs. The family there had failed to make edible butter for two months. Bessie found the old grandfather sitting in the kitchen, agitated and concerned. He became even more distracted and rattled when he realised he had to deal with a very young woman who didn't speak Welsh. He insisted they should go to sort the matter out once and for all, pleading that they go to see the local 'Dyn hysbys' (soothsayer) because the butter was 'bewitched'! His preference was to call for Evan Griffiths of Llangurig, a notable magic healer of those parts, about 15 miles away.

There is no record of the taste or appearance of the bewitched butter effectively but Bessie was not about to allow herself to be at the mercy of a local witchdoctor and the mystic powers of the occult, so she set about making butter the correct way, explaining as she worked, that making good tasting butter was dependent on the quality of milk and that in turn was dependent on the feed given to cattle. She would often recall the experience as she remembered the old man's face when he saw her working the butter - perfect colour, consistency, and texture - into a perfect block. She managed to explain the nature of their problems that was mainly due to the quality of their cattle feed. She told him that the cows should calve more regularly and that they should not give them swedes in their feed, because butter flavour and quality is influenced by the cow's diet. The old man seemed charmed by her personality if not totally convinced by her knowledge.

Bessie's ability to teach and inform was soon recognised and to give her Dairy Department further kudos, she trained students in all the practices to do with milking and making milk products. Two students won prestigious awards at the London Dairy Show and the publicity put her work at Aberystwyth on a high level.

There was a hint of enchantment about Bessie in those early years at Aberystwyth for she had fallen in love with Abel Jones, a Senior Lecturer in the department since 1902, a man of the Welsh soil and a native of Cardiganshire (now Ceredigion). He was tall, dark and handsome with a gentle but strong and practical personality. They were well matched with common interests and a similar background of parents who had struggled to make a living from the land.

Abel was one of eight children, four boys and four girls born to Thomas and Dinah Jones at Llechwedd Farm, in the parish of Llanwenog, south of Lampeter. Thomas was a successful farmer on a mixed farm but his real interest was making the most of the local breed of sheep, the Llanwenog type, a breed indigenous to the Teifi Valley. The breed suited their locality with their distinctive black faces, hardiness and their prolificacy when crossed with other breeds. Thomas Jones was very active in bringing breeders together and was anxious to form a society but his vision and that proposal had to wait until 1957 to be formalised and established.

At that time, the southern triangle of Cardiganshire was known as 'Y Smotyn Du' (The Black Spot), a title which had set it apart due to religion. Unitarianism had flourished in the area and allowed freedom of thought, open mindedness and an individualistic approach coupled with a belief in diversity and equality. It was very different from Methodism with its rules, moral rectitude and closed narrow attitudes. Abel's mother in her younger days had come under the influence of the Unitarian preacher Gwilym Marles who, with tenants of the area, had stood against powerful landowners who had demanded higher rents and ordered them to vote for their chosen candidates at the next general election. They refused and as a result the tenants were locked out of their chapel. Gwilym Marles not to be out-done, or beaten, promptly organised the building of a new chapel. Another preacher, Charles Lloyd, through his stirring sermons also converted many in the area to become Unitarians. So many followed his lead that the Methodists passed a resolution to send missionaries to the area that they dubbed scornfully the belittling title 'Black Spot' as an insult to all Unitarians.

Abel's mother, Dinah, was a devout Unitarian but his father, Thomas, was not so committed (or as devout), having been brought up an Anglican, the church of the State and the feudal landlords. For that reason, the children followed their mother to become Unitarians. Both parents strongly believed in education and that children should be allowed freedom of choice to follow their interests. The farm could not sustain them all and the two older brothers took the decision to emigrate to Australia.

One had suffered from asthma from birth and it was felt a friendlier climate would give him a healthier life-style, but it was that sense of self-belief and inner purpose that was to provide them with a more satisfying living in a new world. The eldest, David struck gold, not from mining, but he did see a golden opportunity to make money in Kalgoorlie where gold had been discovered. It was a desert and the miners needed water. By spending his hard earned savings on a water wagon, he carried water to the parched mines. His Cardiganshire entrepreneurial spirit flourished and he made a fortune from such a simple idea.

Tom, the second brother became a successful dairy farmer in Australia. Meanwhile the three sisters married local farmers in Cardiganshire and the fourth sister Rachel, the youngest, followed a course in pharmacy and became a dispensing chemist. The two remaining brothers living at home were fortunate to receive further education and Abel, the youngest son, went to University College, Bangor to study agriculture. He remained there until his appointment as Senior Lecturer at Aberystwyth to manage a new College acquisition, the farm, Tanygraig, in the parish of Llanfarian. Like Bessie, he travelled everywhere by bike, although the usual form of travel in rural areas at the turn of the century was on horseback. Throughout her life Bessie refused to ride a pony, although she would happily sit in a cart, trap or float to drive one, but when motorcars became the mode of transport, she flatly refused to learn to drive.

Abel and Bessie's romance blossomed and their courtship was a regular subject for departmental gossip and scrutiny but few realised that although Abel was known to College staff by his first Christian name, Bessie always called him Edwin, his second birth name.

Bessie accepted Abel's proposal and their marriage in 1907 was applauded by everyone as a happy event, a Celtic union which also coincided with the arrival of Bryner Jones as a new Professor of Agriculture of great significance. However, at this point, Bessie came up against the protocols of a Welsh University College. The institution did not employ married women and she was forced to resign her post as Dairy Instructor.

The newly married couple set up home as tenants of a smallholding, Crugiau, on the outskirts of Aberystwyth and for them, it was a joy. They shared a common passion for gardening and soon they were growing enough vegetables and fruit for the family and were able to sell the surplus to local shops. Twenty bee-hives lined the walled garden and they also kept two cows, chickens and a pig, so they became almost self-sufficient and always selling the surplus butter, cheese, eggs and honey to local customers. In fact, the small-holding made more money than Bessie had earned as an instructor

Yet all that hard work was noticed and frowned upon, especially when they worked in the garden on Sundays. The influence of the latest Welsh Methodist Revival of 1904 led by Evan Roberts was reaching its peak with its emphasis on social control through religion, preaching eternal torment in hell for those who eschewed nonconformist controls. Working on Sundays was a sin to be punished and the chapel fraternity in Aberystwyth definitely noticed sinners. Abel was a caring humanist from a long line of Unitarians and Bessie came from a religious background of Scottish Presbyterians and was independent and determined. Unperturbed, they carried on working in the garden on Sundays.

Within a year of their marriage a baby girl, Gwyneth, was born and Bessie had her hands full. She found occasional help for the house which gave her time to do some academic work and occasionally she would be invited back to the Department to instruct a class in dairying. She had built up a considerable reputation for her energy and clarity as an instructor and for her sympathetic care for students. The College could ill-afford to neglect such talent on their doorstep. Meanwhile Professor Bryner Jones invited her to contribute a chapter on breeds of poultry for a series of books he was compiling and editing under the title *Livestock of the Farm*. There were six volumes in all, each one devoted to different types and breeds of livestock and, although she constantly maintained she was not an academic, she wrote a detailed analysis of the characteristics of 30 breeds of poultry, plus ducks, geese and turkeys which was published in 1914.

From Orpingtons to Cochin China, Anconas to Rhode Island Reds and the White Wyandotte, Bessie noted the merits of each breed. Other chapters written by different academics detailed the merits of different types of animals and the books became important reference points for farmers and students.

Abel too had been encouraged to write his own comprehensive study of different breeds of livestock and his book *The Selection and Judging of Animals* by A.E.Jones, was also published in 1914, a few months before the hostilities of the first World War had begun. From the beginning of his career he had been interested in livestock breeding and husbandry and his management of the farm Tanygraig was proof of his knowledge and capabilities. In a short time, under strong leadership, the Agricultural Department at Aberystwyth was gaining a reputation for academic studies, research and practical application.

Bessie and Abel's second daughter Dinah, named after her Welsh grandmother, was born in 1911, and from an early age she was soon following her parents, gardening and milking, feeding chickens and collecting eggs. Gwyneth, the eldest was not interested in such pastimes. She preferred books and studies and because of their different interests, there was no real meeting point. As Dinah recalls today, "I didn't get on with my sister. She was an academic through and through, not a bit interested in agriculture."

When Sandy, the third child was born in July 1915, he was named Alexander Llewelyn Lyon Jones. In Sandy Dinah found a soulmate and, as they grew up, they spent a lot of time together. They would visit their Welsh Mamgu (grandmother) at Llanwenog during school holidays and be allowed the freedom to help with the farm work. They enjoyed listening to stories and tales of country life, Welsh customs and folklore. They also travelled to Scotland to stay with their grandparents at Lower Drumgley and, as time went by, they came to experience and understand other systems of farming, in addition to different attitudes and local customs.

Aberystwyth seemed to change overnight after the outbreak of war in 1914. In five months there were 9,000 troops in and around the town but student numbers fell drastically. In 18 months they numbered only 250 students, and 170 of those were women. 'Petticoat Government' was the provocative jibe as more and more committee places were filled by women. But many staff took the opportunity and the time to increase their research activity and Abel Jones joined forces with the College adviser in agriculture, R.G.Stapledon, who, since his arrival in 1912 had already made a detailed ecological survey of many square miles of the county extending from the Cardigan Bay coast to the hills around Plynlimon. Their research partnership now focussed on improving old pastures, especially on the uplands, by manuring, improving the quality of seeds and breaking up swards with mechanical surface treatment. Unfortunately, Stapledon was called away to London to assist with the national government's food-growing campaign but Abel carried on until the end of the war with this aspect of research, coupled with other projects and experiments.

The urgent need to produce more food was intense. Dinah, at that time no more than five or six years old, was well aware of the havoc and damage German submarines were wreaking by firing torpedoes at Merchant Navy ships transporting food to the UK. One day the seriousness of the situation was brought into vivid focus for her, "Mum told me that if the worst came to the worst, we'd have to eat my pet guinea pig," she recalls.

*   *   *   *   *

In 1916 Bessie and Abel had three children under eight years old but that did not prevent Bessie from accepting a government invitation to assist the war effort. The country was desperately short of labour and there was an urgent need to increase food production. In the two years since the beginning of the war, food supplies had dwindled to a level that caused civil unrest and the German U-boat attacks on shipping were scoring too many direct hits. It forced the government to re-think their policies on food production and self-sufficiency but the work-force was seriously depleted. They proposed that women should become directly involved in the war effort and the Board of Trade took the decision to set up a Women's Land Army.

Elizabeth Jones (Bessie) was initially invited to become the Organiser for Cardiganshire but within months she took responsibility for the whole of Wales. Earlier she had been prevented from following her chosen career and her three small children needed care and attention. But she longed to have a taxing job and this work would be challenging, urgent, and at times downright difficult. Abel gave her sympathetic support but there was resistance from farmers, some being openly antagonistic to female workers on the land.

Bessie's work involved mobilising a volunteer work force, selecting and placing suitable candidates on those farms where men had been sent to join the army on the Western Front. Bessie of course was well familiar with resistance and opposition from conservative farmers and by now familiar too with the techniques of persuasion.

She was a good organiser and manager. She was knowledgeable and forthright, able to make decisions and stick to them. She was caring too. Many of her recruits came from urban middle class backgrounds and often she helped inexperienced women to come to terms with new skills in strange surroundings, in new communities far from home. She convinced many a suspicious farmer that these women could learn to milk, weed long rows of swedes and mangolds, and work lethal looking machines for tasks such as hay-making. Bessie earned respect for her practical knowledge but, nevertheless, a few farmers took exception to her robust manner in argument. She countered this by always having time to listen to them and always being civil and courteous.

In less than 18 months they calculated that over 260,000 women in the UK were working as farm labourers. Over 1,000 of them trained as rat catchers, despite the fact that this army of female labour was often labelled by cynics 'The lilac sun-bonnet brigade.' More significantly perhaps, they were also subsequently referred to as the 'forgotten army' once war was over.

There were posters everywhere in villages, towns and cities encouraging young women to join up but nothing as direct or as forceful as the iconic poster of Lord Kitchener's finger pointing his command, 'Your Country Needs You'. Instead posters for women showed a tranquil rural scene with a woman ploughing an open field. She holds the handles daintily as a pair of shire horses plod and pull the plough towards the sunset, the sun's rays like searchlights highlighting the sky. The perfect backdrop for a rather whispy sort of woman - she almost deserves to be called a lady – dressed in her regulatory floppy hat, her knee length coat lifted enticingly by an imagined breeze. Boots and leggings delicately walk the furrow, the plough steady and straight as three or four seagulls hover above waiting for worms to surface when the tilth is turned. The caption reads, in capital letters, 'GOD SPEED THE PLOUGH AND THE WOMAN WHO DRIVES IT,' a strap-line which must have been written by a bored city civil servant far removed from farming practices, for in those long ago days, no one 'drove' a plough, they followed it.

Every Women's Land Army (WLA) recruit was given a uniform reflecting the image in the poster – brown corduroy trousers, green jerseys and leggings, a mackintosh, hob nailed boots and a broad brimmed, shapeless WLA floppy hat. There were regular complaints from the fashion conscious recruits. One constant complaint was that the boots were heavy and never really kept their feet dry. Water seeped in through the lace holes even in summer when heavy morning dew formed on the grass.

Hilda Vaughan the recruitment officer in Brecon in a rousing speech to young women in Newtown said, "I am putting before you the disadvantages of the life. Long hours, hard work, poor pay! After you get your board and lodge, a shilling a day perhaps." Then she offered something special adding to the monetary reward, "Good health, good sleep and good complexions. I need volunteers!"

One of Bessie's major concerns during her time as the WLA Director for Wales was that young girls who were experiencing country life for the first time would be exposed to disease on farms. The scourge of the time, tuberculosis in cattle, was rife in West Wales, and the number dying from 'the consumption' was increasing year by year. She often recalled a young girl she interviewed, a doctor's daughter from Cardiff who Bessie believed was not robust enough to survive the rigours of farming life. She invited her to stay at her home Crugiau to work as a land girl on the small-holding but unfortunately, an outbreak of severe flu swept through the land and the young girl became a victim and, despite careful nursing, she died. Her death affected Bessie deeply. She felt she had failed the girl's family and herself. It was a low point at a time when she and Abel were so busy, with the both Land Army work and the University Agricultural Department.

Dinah, their daughter recalls those years, "It was hectic. We as children hardly saw them. But there was never any disharmony in the home."

As the war ended, Bessie was pregnant with their fourth child. In 1917 Abel's cousin Dinah, who had also qualified as a Dairy Instructor, joined the Aberystwyth Department and, when the war ended, she and Bessie became co-workers and close friends. Bessie was not a staff member but because of a shortage of teachers, lecturers and instructors, the college authorities waived protocols and engaged anyone who was trained and experienced.

The war had strongly influenced the importance of women workers and immediately following the Armistice in 1918, women over the age of 30 were enfranchised by law. They had won the right to vote. It took another ten years (1928) to achieve parity with men, but there was a widely held view that the vote had been given to women as a reward for their services during the war.

The right to vote had not come easily. Mrs Emily Pankhurst and her followers led the fight for women's suffrage and were imprisoned many times for their acts of civil disobedience and damage to property. It was not quite the new dawn of opportunity in the work place either. Old patriarchal attitudes were deeply ingrained and women were expected to resume their roles as wives, mothers and dutiful daughters.

Thankfully Abel did not think that way. He saw their marriage as a partnership and he was delighted when Bessie's work as Director of the WLA was rewarded with the MBE. He continued to give her as many opportunities as possible and she, and his cousin Dinah, travelled to Denmark to see for themselves how the Danes managed their farming community and how their dairy practices could be applied in Wales. It was to be a worthwhile educative process and a new emphasis for extra-mural courses.

They returned, crossing the channel in a storm, with the ship tossing in high waves and weaving to avoid mines left by German U-boats. Dinah stood on deck ready to face anything the sea threw at her but a pregnant Bessie retreated down below to lie down. Later and sadly within months of the birth, David her fourth child, died of flu. Bessie was distraught and blamed herself because the baby had never really had time to build up his immune system.

But six months later there was an opportunity for a family celebration. Professor Bryner Jones announced his resignation as Head of Department. He had been invited to become Assistant Secretary to the Government's Board of Agriculture. The post of Professor of Agriculture at Aberystwyth was advertised and from a large field of applicants, Abel Edwin Jones was promoted to the Chair to lead the department. He had that rare quality of combining the intellect of an academic and the eminently practical mind of a practising farmer, qualities that endeared him to the farming community.

Yet Bessie's joy and pleasure at her husband's success was soon tempered when she became seriously ill with an infection and the respected local doctor, Dr Ellis failed to prescribe a cure. The family in Scotland were seriously concerned at her weakening condition and begged Abel to allow them to take her to see a naturopath in Edinburgh, their words ringing in his ears, "Don't let the medicals interfere with our Bess, we'll get her through this."

And this they did, because the family believed that curative power comes from the healing power of nature, which calls for self-discipline, motivation and courage to make life-style adjustments and the will-power to sustain changes. No quick fixes from pills and potions but a process of regeneration that could only come from natural recuperation. Bessie's eventual recovery was slow but complete, for those qualities needed to sustain a healthy life-style she had in abundance.

The experience again also re-inforced her beliefs in the way food should be produced. A healthy soil produced healthy food products but during the war years there had been continuing political and commercial pressure for farmers to increase production through the use of inorganic manures, weedkillers and pesticides on crops. In Bessie's opinion the long term effects of such practices could not be determined and she was totally opposed to the intellectual argument, based on the Darwinian theory that this was only a reflection of man's fight to dominate nature.

Abel too maintained that domination was not part of the equation. He knew that qualitative research would provide some of the answers to questions such as how the soil for growing pastures and meadows, arable and root crops could be enhanced. There was an urgent need to improve the quality of seed mixtures and to devise new systems of managing grassland and grazing for sheep and cattle.

Within a few months of taking the Chair, Abel welcomed George Stapledon back to Aberystwyth from his Government war work to take up a new post, the Chair of Agricultural Botany and to direct a new establishment, The Welsh Plant Breeding Station. Under Stapledon's guidance during the next three decades, the work of young pioneering scientists at the station, the only scientific research institute in Wales, gained an international reputation.

A true visionary, Stapledon was one of the few men who inaugurated a revolution and lived to see it become an accepted tradition. His mission to improve grasslands would often be illustrated with a quote from Dean Swift in Gulliver's Travels: *'Whoever could make two ears of corn or two blades of grass to grow upon a spot where only one grew before, would deserve better of mankind and do more essential service to his country than the whole race of politicians put together.'*

Abel was to work closely with Stapledon, especially on the practical side of managing grassland and getting the best out of the land. They formed a deep friendship as they developed their ideas, bouncing them off each other often well into the night and frequently causing upsets and anger in their home-life. Bessie thought Abel should be at home gardening at Crugiau and Mrs Stapledon thought her husband should be doing more constructive work rather than wasting time 'gossiping'. But these conversations were of real importance as the College had acquired a 150 acre farm in the Clarach Valley, three miles north of Aberystwyth. The link between scientific research in the laboratory could find a practical application at Nantcellan Farm that was destined to be Abel and Bessie's new home. It was in an ideal location with good south facing land but the house and buildings needed modernising. They would manage the farm and plan its development, in addition to directing Departmental activities, putting the emphasis on degree courses and post-graduate research. But as a first priority, a new cowshed and dairy was built to house 40 dairy cows, piped water was installed to the house and buildings and a powerful generator commissioned to provide electricity. It was to be a mixed farm, typical of many Welsh farms, but the emphasis without doubt was to be milk production. Yet the excitement of setting up a new enterprise was tempered with a little sadness. Leaving Crugiau, the small-holding that had been their home for the first twelve years of their marriage was a wrench, but the wide lawns and borders at Nantcellan plus the large kitchen garden and orchard would become an absorbing interest and a challenge.

*   *   *   *   *

These were busy and remarkable times. The post-war years presented particular problems in terms of farm labour, but there was a significant increase in the number of students. The ground rules had been established for new degree courses; stocking the farm was completed in two years; and research was underway into cropping, rotational grazing and animal husbandry.

This was the time when their marriage became a partnership in every sense of the word and Bessie's experience was paramount. The farm was run as a commercial enterprise and she was to take charge of the dairy herd and administer the needs of the employees working directly on the farm. Bessie was in her element. She kept detailed records of the yield from every cow, the length of lactation, how much feed and hay was used on a daily and weekly basis, in addition to organising and cajoling everyone to give a little more effort.

She was a disciplinarian too and for her there had to be a structure and an order of work for the day. Rarely did anyone deviate without first consulting Bessie, the 'boss'. The emphasis on milk production brought more students to Aberystwyth to study dairying. Milk from the Nantcellan herd was taken to the College by nine in the morning so that cheese and butter-making sessions could get underway.

Dinah, by now eleven years old, had already set her mind on being a farmer. She had milked by hand the two cows at Crugiau since she was five years old, and her mother persuaded her to help with the morning milking at Nantcellan because the men were not always reliable, or, as Dinah recalls,

"I helped with the milking at a very early age because men never liked milking. They only got interested when machines came in. Mother challenged me to get up at six o'clock every morning before school. And then she rewarded me with a promise that she would take me to compete at the London Dairy Show. She entered me for the class for the under 18 milking competition when I was 12 and I won! Well, I had been well taught. I knew how to wash a cow for hygiene and cleanliness. I knew how to approach a cow for milking and which teats to milk first. I was practised in all those tasks. I got first prize and £10 pocket money. That was a lot of money then. Funnily enough it was a Scots girl who won the Supreme Championship. That was in 1923."

However just a year later, family tragedy struck and Abel was to die of leukaemia. Academically he was at the top of his prowess but physically he had been coping with fever, weakness and fatigue for almost a year and when the diagnosis was given, they knew it would be fatal. Little could be done except for doses of Arsenic Trioxide to combat the march of white blood cells in his blood. Bessie took him to Buxton for three months to see if the air and curative powers of the spa waters would help his fevers and fatigue. Dinah, his cousin, came several times a week to spend time with him and Dinah, his daughter, remembers that despite his debilitating illness, he kept his sense of humour and his powers of observation.

Back home, he would always ask her about her days at school and especially about activities on the farm. A rather weakling calf had been born, but Dinah kept that news to herself, not wanting to bother him. Everyday she went into his room to talk about her work at school and her activities on the farm, and one day he asked, "How's the calf today?"
"Why do you want to know?" she asked.
"Because you haven't talked about it, and that's not like you," said Abel.
There was a pause as Dinah failed to answer,
"It's dead isn't it?" he asked quietly.
And it was.

*   *   *   *   *

Abel died on February 12th 1924 and Dinah recalls those dark days of loss and grief and the anger she felt at the prolonged treatment using arsenic products her father received from the medicals. It confirmed in her mind that a natural treatment was the most effective way to cope with illness and disease.

Bessie was bereft. She had lost her husband of 17 years and she would have to move from her home because Nantcellan was a college farm. Her three children were young, Gwyneth the eldest was just 16, and she would have to find work. It called for all Bessie's reserves of willpower, discipline and energy to survive.

The college authorities were benign and encouraged her to stay in the house for at least a year. In fact she stayed 18 months, time to overcome the sharpness of grief and to formulate a plan of action. Her mother-in-law was a tower of strength. Bessie talked at length to her because she had decided she wanted to farm and Dinah Jones of Llanwenog was kind, wise and pragmatic. Bessie respected her views and counsel, while her own family, in particular her elder brother Dave, attempted to persuade her to return to Scotland. "You'll never scratch a livelihood here," he said.

The quality of land in the Clarach Valley was different from that in Strathmore. In truth he encouraged Bessie to return to teaching. Yet Bessie had spent 24 years in Wales and the Welsh had accepted her.

According to her daughter Dinah, "Mother used to say, the Welsh people had far more appreciation of women and the contribution they made. That's why she didn't go back to Scotland. She would never have farmed on her own in Scotland."

Fortunately, the tenancy of a 53 acre farm Nantllan in the Clarach Valley next to Nantcellan became available and Abel's parents gave her the first down-payment on a mortgage for her new home and business venture.

One of the few letters she wrote to her mother-in-law has survived in her daughter Dinah's safe-keeping and in it she describes her worries about money, the need for help on the farm and how to pay for stock. It reads: *'I thought I could manage by myself and save some money, but I am afraid it would be too much for me. A girl from North Wales whom I knew as a land girl is coming next week.'*

Meanwhile her brother Dave was by now supportive. *'I have discussed Nantllan with Dave. He thought it was very kind of you to lend me that money to buy Nantllan. Then if I wanted any more for stocking, he would help me. I must think about getting the deeds made out and then I can make a will putting things right for the bairns.'*

Then she goes on to mention one of the bairns, Dinah, and her intention of sending her to a girls' public school. *'I am hoping to*

send Dinah to Dr Williams School at Dolgellau next year. Edwin
(Abel) wanted her to go and I think it is only fair that she should go.'

And almost at the end of the eight page letter, after underlining
the interest of 5% she would pay on the £500 loan, she writes:
'I do not know how to thank you for all you have done for me. You
have been better than my own flesh and blood. When are you
coming up again? With love. Yours Bess.'

Bessie's resolute character shines through the writing. She's
honest about the tough problems facing her, a warmth in her cares
and hopes for the children and a hint of excitement and tenacity
about her future in farming. She admired Abel's mother, known
to the children as 'our Welsh Mam-gu,' perhaps more than her
own mother and increasingly she came to rely on her advice.

There were others too in the community who gave her tangible
support. When H.P. Edwards the butcher at Aberystwyth heard
that Bessie had set her mind on developing a dairy farm and
wanted to introduce a milk round in the town, he offered to buy
cows 'on tick' for her. She made just one stipulation – that every
cow should be tested for tuberculosis so that when she began
selling milk, it would be the first bottled Grade A Tuberculin
Attested milk in the area. Her first journey in 1926 driving a pony
and milk float filled with bottled milk - which she had bottled
herself - was a success and the round grew but Bessie knew there
was much more to be done. She had set herself a long term plan

to concentrate on production of high quality milk and within months she had paid H.P Edwards for the cows, a mixture of two breeds, Ayrshires and Shorthorns. She would also practise her belief in natural, organic farming by never using inorganic fertilisers or pesticides on her land. Nantllan was to become the first of the family tradition.

Bessie took time to decide on a permanent breed of cattle, one which would yield a rich quality product. Based on her observations on the daily milk round, she had realised it was the deep cream line on the bottle of milk that attracted customers and she soon settled on a Channel Island breed, the Guernsey. Her judgement was coloured by another factor. Despite their rather delicate image, Bessie knew Guernseys to be hardy and adaptable, a breed well used to Atlantic storms and cold rain as the indigenous cattle of a small windswept island. She calculated they would do well in a similar environment on the shores of Cardigan Bay. She sold the Shorthorns and true to her Scottish background, kept the Ayrshires. They converted grass into milk efficiently, were hardy and the composition of their milk was ideally suited for the production of butter and cheese.

Bessie travelled by train to Reading to attend a well known Guernsey cattle sale where she bought about ten cows which would form the basis of her dairy herd and be enough to fill one railway goods wagon. They duly arrived safely at Bow Street station following an eight hour journey and where Dinah, her daughter, was waiting to help drive them two miles on foot to Nantllan. The Guernsey cattle survived and thrived on their new pastures and were kept out night and day, summer and winter. The Ayrshires by comparison, indigenous to northern areas and climate, seemed much more delicate. They searched for shelter under trees and hedges when the wind blew from the sea and they were always wintered indoors at night.

Local farmers thought her farming practices eccentric and were convinced that she would never make a success of the enterprise. The most popular breed of cattle of those times in Wales was the dual-purpose Shorthorn, kept for the production of milk and meat. They had been the mainstay of Welsh agriculture for many decades. They were hardy, yet they were always kept indoors during winter months and their milk was only of average quality. Furthermore, when they saw Bessie spreading seaweed to enrich the soil, a system practised by the Channel Islanders, they could hardly believe their eyes. Years later, analysis proved that milk from the Nantllan herd was not only rich and creamy, but it was naturally high in protein and calcium and had more vitamins and total milk solids than milk from any other breed.

The children were growing up and when the move to Nantllan took place, Gwyneth, the eldest had entered the University College at Aberystwyth to study Botany and Zoology. She was bright and an academic through and through like her Scotch Granny, according to her sister, Dinah, 'very outspoken too, just like my mother,' and when it came to choosing one subject for her degree course, Gwyneth's choice was Zoology but her mother persuaded her to concentrate on Botany.

Dr Lily Newton, a revered name in academic scientific circles had just taken over the department and unfortunately, Gwyneth did not exactly see eye to eye with her. In her final degree grading, she was given a Third which left her bruised when so much was expected of her. However, George Stapledon gave her a job at the Plant Breeding Station and she remained there until she married a brilliant fellow student, a geographer, Estyn Evans, who went on to become Vice-Chancellor of Queen's University, Belfast.

As agreed, Dinah went to the Dr Williams School for Girls at Dolgellau but for one year only. Bessie could not afford the school fees so Dinah came home to complete her schooldays at Ardwyn Grammar School. The added bonus for her was to return to the farm to help her mother and to join one of the agricultural short courses at the University. Her brother Sandy the youngest, also intended making his living on the land when he left school, but his main interest, like his Scottish grandfather, was machinery.

Bessie was working hard, from dawn until ten at night every day and was slowly achieving her goals. Farmers wives thought her to be different, an enigma to be admired, envied, or privately ridiculed. As ever, she remained uninterested in clothes and fashion.

"She had one tweed outfit that seemed to have lasted years – classical, structured and very practical," recalls Dinah. "And she always wore a hat, a sort of cloche, but that was because she didn't have a lot of hair, like her mother before her. Once I saw my Granny in Scotland without a wig and then I saw Granny with a wig. I had a terrible shock."

The emphasis on farm work was a necessity to make a living but it did not imply a neglect of home comforts. The house was well furnished and orderly. Bessie had a strong love of Welsh furniture which she kept well polished and she was a good cook. Colin Evans her nephew, Gwyneth's son, spent two years training with her in later years and he remembers her cooking. Her days always began in true Scottish fashion, with a bowl of porridge and Guernsey cream and her meals were simple and tasty. She would pull out all the stops on threshing days when eleven or more strong men from the local community would sit down for lunch of lamb stew, swedes, carrots and jacket potatoes followed by the most wonderful creamy rice pudding.

Most of the time Bessie was on her own doing a man's job. Any man who questioned her judgement, she would cut them down to size in a flash. Yet her workmen had a good working relationship with her. They knew she was a practical person as well as a theorist. She wasn't a boss who dictated her instructions, she worked alongside her men, and if she wasn't able to be there, she would demonstrate how the job should be done. Colin remembers her as an encouraging teacher, practical and thorough, more often than not, teaching by example, but, "If I contradicted her point of view, it caused displeasure, not a put down and a discussion to make me see sense."

She often engaged men from Scotland who came highly recommended by Dave and her brothers for their skills and affinity with livestock husbandry. One or two stayed a long time, trusted and loyal, but just occasionally there would be signs of indiscipline especially at weekends. There was one occasion when Bessie had been negotiating working hours with the Union and was perfectly willing to comply with the new agreement but she stipulated that she needed cover for milking at weekends. The men were encouraged to draw up a rota and one particular worker, not milking, went off to Aberystwyth for the Saturday afternoon. He enjoyed himself drinking too much Welsh beer and did not return home. A neighbour had found him leaning on, or perhaps wrapped around, a lamp-post in front of the station singing raucously at the top of his voice, 'The Bonnie Bonnie Banks of Loch Lomond.' The neighbour helped him to the promenade and showed him the coastal path over Constitution

Hill to Clarach beach, leaving him to his own devices on the narrow rocky path above the sea.

That kind of behaviour did not please Bessie and she told him in no uncertain manner, "I hear you've been disgracing the name of Scotland. If that's the way you behave, you will be working every Saturday."

That was her way of dealing with human frailties. Deal with it directly and then forget about it.

She often trained young people, giving them an opportunity. One local young man called Billy had always caused concern to his parents and his mother pleaded with Bessie to give him a trial working on the farm. She agreed, but first, she gave him a lesson on demeanour, attitude and behaviour, what was expected of him and that it was time he grew up to take responsibility. "It is time to become a man," she told him firmly.

Billy went out of the door and as he left, he turned to Bessie, stretching himself to full height said, "Mrs Jones, I'm going to be a man. A stockman."

The bull was in the yard, seemingly attacking the resident stockman and Billy, with the words of promise he had just spoken ringing in his ears, tried to interfere with a strong, angry bull and was immediately tossed and gored. He died later from his wounds and it was a tragic incident that affected everyone deeply. Bessie more than anyone, for her advice, honestly given, had prompted a huge human tragedy.

As a codicil to the distressing incident, Billy was known locally as 'Billy Two-Time' because he always carried two watches, one on his wrist and the other in his top pocket tied to the lapel button hole. There was never any doubt that Billy knew the correct time for he would always check both. On the day of the accident his pocket watch stopped at the exact second he was tossed by the bull.

Dinah was at school in Aberystwyth that day but she remembers the incident because she had unwittingly presaged events. She had been given a bundle of peacock feathers which she had carefully arranged and placed on a lintel above the fireplace before leaving for school. She returned in the late afternoon and a group of children stopped her at the village crossroads to tell her they had heard of a terrible accident and that Dinah was somehow to blame because she had brought peacock feathers into the house. She raced home, scooped up the feathers and threw them on the fire, too late to save Billy but at least to avoid further accidents.

Dinah recalls her mother comforted her saying that people said feathers were a sign of bad luck, an omen, a superstition, nothing more but because of the power of old country supersititions, she too, had thought of burning them.

Despite being structured and disciplined, coupled with a liking for order at work, Bessie was inventive and an entrepreneur. The milk round had shown that she preferred to sell her products direct to the customer, mainly milk, cream and eggs, but one Christmas, at market time she caused a sensation, selling early lamb and broccoli. Nantllan was a mixed farm with an emphasis on milk production but when the Milk Marketing Board (MMB) was established in 1933, Bessie was highly critical and openly spoke her mind saying, "It will suppress people's initiative. It will protect them from the market place which has always been a farming tradition."

For others, the Board gave confidence to a depressed industry providing steadier prices and guaranteed collection, distribution and markets. Those guarantees appealed to the farming community and the number of farmers who concentrated on milk production increased year by year. In 1934 there were 9,000 milk producers in Wales. Ten years later that number had almost trebled.

Bessie remained sceptical. "The big farmer could always out-vote the little man," she maintained and when she saw the number of Friesian cows increasing she said caustically of the quality of milk they produced, "Friesians are nothing but water-barrels."

She feared that her rich, creamy milk would be mixed with inferior quality milk, and worse, that milk from herds likely to be carrying tuberculosis would be mixed with clean milk when the collecting lorries emptied their churns into huge tanks of milk at the Felinfach and Pont Llanio creameries. But within a short time, a testing system was in place, strict guidelines issued and a campaign launched to force West Wales dairy herds to become tuberculosis free.

Bessie's inventiveness as a means of overcoming seemingly insurmountable problems was highlighted during a heavy snow storm in 1937. Roads were closed, farms were cut off and Bessie failed to deliver milk to her customers. Undaunted, she organised local fishermen to come to her rescue. The following morning they landed their boats on nearby Clarach beach, loaded the crates of bottled milk and cream and Bessie sailed her lactic cargo into the neighbouring Aberystwyth harbour. Milk was delivered to grateful customers coupled with a complimentary pot of cream produced from the milk she had failed to deliver the previous day.

A lifestyle working from dawn to dusk brought its financial returns and finally Bessie was able to buy Glanymor, a farm between Nantllan and the sea. More acres of land gave her greater flexibility and opportunities to diversify. She decided to venture into tourism and bought two small caravans and a double decker bus which she adapted into a two storey mobile home. (Although it wasn't exactly mobile, the wheels having been removed for safety. This was not to be conventional tourism!). Bessie had realised that the gap between town and country was widening and also, the economic depression of the 1930s prevented those out of work from having the opportunity to enjoy cheap holidays. Bessie began a scheme which combined work and leisure for townspeople. In return for undertaking light work on the farm in the mornings, they could have free accommodation and afternoons to relax in the sun and the sea.

Another aspect of her humanitarianism was her kindness to tramps, people who were shunned by the majority, but who would work with a will in return for food and lodgings. Occasionally she had as many as four sleeping in the barn, the following morning awaiting a hearty breakfast and she had her regular callers. They were given their tasks and in return she gave them shelter and when the task was completed, they would move on. There were one or two who abused her kindness and she wouldn't be afraid to tell them so, but she accepted there were individuals in society who didn't have the ability or the means to do what society expected them to do. Bessie could never turn her back on them.

The years since Abel died had not been easy, not least developing the farm and following beliefs that made her seem at odds with the prevailing agricultural wisdom of the 1920s and 1930s.

Economic depression, falling land prices, the threat of a second World War pointed the way for greater efficiency and higher productivity, but Bessie refused to compromise her belief in maintaining natural products of high quality.

Celebrating her 50th birthday in 1939, she looked to the future to determine which of her bairns would take over from her. It was to be Dinah.

*　*　*　*　*

DINAH

DINAH

"I always wanted to farm. I remember being given a task at school, I think it was for the Eleven Plus exam, to write an essay. They asked, what do you want to do when you grow up and I remember writing 'I want to be a farmer', telling them all about the cows. Nothing deflected me then and nothing has deflected me since."

Dinah today is an active 97 year old, quick and animated with an alert, smooth skinned face dominated by smiles. She's short and slim, keeps herself as fit as possible, takes a cold bath every morning, walks the fields every day and eats natural food from organic produce. She is passionately interested and involved in farming policies and agricultural politics. In conversation she is direct and her blue eyes become steely when she discusses topics such as GM crops or blatant intensive farming methods and the role of women in agriculture.

Dinah's life after she completed a short course in agriculture was closely intertwined with that of her mother. Asked if she was bright at school, she retorts,

"Well, I held my own."

"Do you regret not taking the degree course at the University?"

"Not really, Mother seems to have been determined that I would farm."

"Did you always agree with her when you were farming?"

"Oh no, but she was good. Mind she was always sceptical of the academics, even though she married one."

There's pride and admiration in her voice as Dinah recalls her mother's guidance and care, especially the tough times following Abel's death. Dinah was twelve years old when he died and it was those conversations between father and daughter, the observations, impressions and stories as they walked round the sheep, working the dogs in the fields of Crugiau and Nantcellan that remain vivid in her mind. He had always been a busy man but without fail, he made time to listen. His death affected her deeply and even today, her eyes well up and her voice breaks as she talks about him, especially when the suffering became more acute and the lethargy weakened his spirit.

Her mother never fussed over her. "She was not a 'fuss' kind of woman. She got you to do things and you just got on with it," but Dinah acknowledges, her voice softening as she recalls the sad events of 1924, "My mother had a hard time when my father died."

Dinah speaks of her childhood with happiness, not all that interested in schoolwork but observing and listening to all matters to do with agriculture as she learnt all the skills of livestock husbandry. Her parents put particular emphasis on education and that was one of the reasons her father wished her to go to the private school for girls, the revered Dr Williams School at Dolgellau, celebrated and acclaimed by parents for its educational standards and feared by young girls for the stringency of its discipline and the austere surroundings. Dinah spent one year there and the twelve months seemed to pass without incident or a major memory to recall, other than missing the farm and pining for the cows. When prompted about the boarding school, she said, "It did open my eyes to the lives of other girls, to other attitudes, and from other backgrounds. I suppose it did me some good."

Asked how much of a Scot she felt, she says, "I suppose half and half, but I think I'm more like my Welsh Mam-gu, my father's mother. You see Mother had education, Mam-gu did not. She was a practical woman and enjoyed farming but they both firmly believed in the value of a good education."

Dinah joined her mother on the farm in 1930 and for the next decade their lives together as mother and daughter became close, ever dependent on each other, but at work, they maintained the teacher/pupil relationship. She knew her mother to be very disciplined with great application. "What she said usually worked you know. That never bothered me," says Dinah.

It would be easy to believe that Dinah subjugated her own views and feelings, living in her mother's shadow, but she was developing ideas of her own and with growing confidence was able to express them without rancour but in a direct manner. She accepted Bessie's system of farming as the correct husbandry to care for animals, to produce food from the land without unnatural additives and to sell natural products of quality. She was learning her skills and craft on the land and the experience of working with animals, dairy cattle in particular, gave her a deep insight into breeding programmes and the quality and characteristics needed to make the right selections for their herd.

These were difficult times in agriculture where the effect of an acute recession and a depressed economy had taken its toll. Land values slumped and prices fell, labour was scarce and also expensive. Farmers faced ruin, changing to a system that would give them hope of covering their production costs was the only solution for survival. It was a time of dereliction and deterioration on many farms but research into ways of improving farm crops and livestock was gathering momentum. Many farmers turned to milk production and even at four pence a gallon or less, selling milk gave better returns than a combination of stock rearing, store cattle and butter-making. Bessie had seen this coming when she began farming on her own at Nantllan. She had set up her round selling milk directly to the customer and by the time Dinah joined her, they were slowly developing and increasing their dairy herd of Ayrshires and Guernseys. They were also aware that to increase the number of cattle and their productivity, they would need better pastures and research into ways of improving grassland was taking place on their doorstep.

George Stapledon, and his scientists at the Aberystwyth Plant Breeding Station were developing plant breeding techniques to produce leafier strains of grasses. That line of research into improving grazing pastures was innovative and had not been attempted before in any other country. Scientists at the station studied the comparison between wild and cultivated grass types and by cross-pollinating one with the other eventually produced new and nutritious leafy strains of grasses and clovers with titles such as S23 Perennial Ryegrass, S 48 Timothy, S 143 Cocksfoot and S100 White Clover. These newly bred strains were then tested in field conditions. It was a slow process during the 1930s, but it allowed further practical studies to demonstrate how effective management of pastures and swards could increase productivity. Stapledon had also turned his attention to the fertility of upland pastures, land 500 feet above sea-level, which was the classification of much of the hinterland of Wales. Depopulation had gathered pace after the first World War and this was an attempt to make the hills and moors more productive, improve the rural economy and sustain communities.

Many of the practical studies, including soil testing and the benefits of management systems such as rotational grazing were carried out at their old home, the college farm, Nantcellan, and by the beginning of 1939 with the fears of another World War looming, the demand for the country to be self-sufficient was inevitable. The emphasis had definitely turned to milk production and improving grassland. A herd of cows had become the basis for a farm's prosperity and the goal was not to be so dependent on imported feed. There were demonstrations and meetings with farmers up and down the land, not only showing the merits of new grass varieties and strains, but the management of new leys and swards, conserving leafy grass in good condition as hay and silage for winter feed.

Bessie and Dinah carried on as before, refusing to intensify their production by adding inorganic fertilisers on their land at Nantllan and Glanymor. They were careful not to over-stock and not to over-graze their pastures, allowing time for fields to regenerate. Their grassland management included a measure of rotational grazing and although their seed mixtures would include the correct proportions of new leafy grass strains with white or red clovers, they resisted the call to intensify by artificial means their farming practices. Clovers and other legumes such as peas and beans were vital to produce successful grazing pastures. They are the soil's natural fertiliser. Through nodules on their roots they have the ability to fix atmospheric nitrogen in the soil and this is the basic ingredient of protein. When these pastures are disturbed by cutting or grazing, the roots and nodules break down and decay and the nitrogen is then released into the soil to benefit other plants.

As the number of dairy herds increased, doubling in the 1930s, so the Milk Marketing Board built creameries at Pont Llanio, Felinfach and Llangadog. They became the collecting points for milk from small and large farms and also acted as distribution centres for fresh milk to urban centres. Surplus milk was also turned into butter and cheese there.

But Nantllan continued to sell their product directly to their customers locally in Aberystwyth. They firmly believed that milk of high quality with its nutritious balance of elements should not be sacrificed in the quest for high yields. They continued to maintain the balanced natural way which many locals referred to as 'muck and magic'. Year by year milk production increased, not dramatically but steadily in relation to the quality of cattle and the amount of feed they could produce on the farm. They kept careful lactation records of individual cows so that they could track yields and production progress. They were well aware of the growing importance of vitamins in a balanced feed. Also mineral trace elements such as cobalt, zinc or magnesium, and how a deficiency could cause a loss of condition and animal disease. So Dinah and her mother continued to spread seaweed collected from the beach as a valuable mineral supplement to enrich pastures.

Dinah was developing a good eye and knowledge of breeding characteristics and no doubt she would have liked to develop a pedigree line of Guernsey cattle but her mother, who still had a liking for the Ayrshires, had decided to maintain a mixed commercial herd for milk production. The two cattle breeds seemed to complement each other within the dairy herd.

In the mid 1930s, the neighbouring farm, Glanymor bordering the sea, had become available and to increase their acreage they bought it. Dinah and Bessie moved to live in the Glanymor farmhouse, almost on the sea-shore, leaving Sandy in Nantllan. He was tall, strong, well built, a golden head of hair and blue eyes and, at the age of 21, every woman in the Clarach Valley fancied him. Turning his thoughts to other matters, such as making a living, following in his Scottish grandfather's footsteps, he focused his attention to machinery and farm contracting.

The face of agriculture was rapidly changing as tractor power replaced horse power and when the small grey Ferguson tractor (the 'Fergie') came on the market, the mechanical revolution was complete. Ideally suited to small Welsh farms, it was strong, manoeuvrable and flexible. The pace of life quickened and farmers changed from grooming and polishing horse livery to become engineers and mechanics, thereby almost overnight enabling them to accomplish much more in a working day.

Sandy bought his first tractor, a Fordson, for £140, a much more powerful machine than the Ferguson and the spirit of the entrepreneur and the magic of mechanics turned a childhood dream into reality. The Fordson with its huge spade lugg wheels heralded Sandy's new contracting business. He began ploughing with a larger plough, two or three furrows at a time, so much more powerful and speedier than the horse drawn single furrow.

But with a machine of such great speed and power came the accidents. Working on a farm, Riwel Uchaf near Bow Street, one day he overturned both the tractor and the trailer. George Fletcher sitting in the trailer was thrown some 30 yards breaking ribs and his collar bone and Sandy was trapped unconscious underneath the tractor. The two farmers from Riwel Uchaf and Isaf, Alfred Edwards and William Evans ran to the scene. The weight and power of the monster tractor almost overwhelmed them, but they managed to remove the trailer, and William Evans decided when he saw Sandy's face turning blue they could no longer delay matters. He placed himself strategically, legs apart, knees bent, shirt sleeves rolled up and placed his large hands underneath the machine. Then he flexed his muscles and with a mighty heave, that would have done credit to an Olympic weightlifter, he lifted the tractor just high enough and long enough for Alfred Edwards to pull Sandy free. Alfred knew something of first-aid and Sandy recovered his colour without serious injuries, but shaken and bruised. George took a long time to recover from his fractures and William Evans, it was said, was never the same man again following his feat of lifting the tractor.

Next, Sandy bought a Caterpillar, a safer and stronger machine for hilly ground, plus a two furrow plough that could work on steep slopes covered with bracken and heather. In the first year, working day and night he ploughed 2000 acres for the asking price of 15 shillings an acre. Sandy's business was well and truly launched.

A year later Dinah and her aunt Rachel left the farm to join a three week tour to the USSR led by Sir John Russell, Director of Rothamsted Scientific Institute. Aunty Rachel was Abel's youngest sister, a pharmacist who had taken an active interest in sociological matters. She had become a member of the Le Play Society, established in the 1920s in honour of the French engineer, Frederic Le Play for his detailed surveys and field work in sociology and geography. The society also promoted good relations between countries by organising educational tours and, although Bessie was too busy to leave the farm, she believed that Dinah would benefit from the experience and her sister-in-law, Rachel, would be the ideal companion for the journey.

Sir John travelled extensively and was respected for his advice and wise counsel. He had been a regular visitor to Russia since 1930 when he attended the International Society of Soil Science Congress in Leningrad and Moscow. He had kept in close touch with Bessie ever since meeting her when she arrived at Aberystwyth from Scotland, and, in later years he would often come to the University College as a member of the Council. This was to be his third major tour to Russia. He believed Dinah and her aunt would profit from experiencing a new system of farming and different political and social attitudes. Following the Russian revolution there had been sweeping changes in the agricultural organisation with landowners liquidated, their houses and estates taken over by the state. There was much to take in.

In 1937 their 24-day tour began in Moscow, then on to the Volga region, the Ukraine and Armenia but by the late 1930s there had been many changes and visitors' movement was restricted. Collective farming was also far advanced – a farm in the Caucuses covered 500,000 acres and most of the directors were politicians.

In the early revolutionary days the collective ideology was forced on farms. Peasants had to give up their land, implements, and livestock to the collective. Anyone who objected was noted and punished, but such was the unrest that by 1937, Stalin promised that each peasant could keep one cow. It was only after a further period of unrest that rules and controls were relaxed, when peasants were told they could have a piece of land of their own to farm but they should work at least 100 days a year on the collective. In a show of individuality and independence, peasants mostly ignored the needs of the state and would always choose days that best suited them, but the law was again stiffened in an attempt to maintain the Communist ideology.

Dinah was deeply impressed by the exceptionally dedicated farmers of the Ukraine who had good soil to work from but their battle for independence was suffocating their aspirations and it was one of the worst aspects of the visit. The volume and intensity of authoritarian propaganda had a cumulative effect and the abiding memory of that long visit for Dinah and her aunt was the sight of posters on every wall and free space aimed at those working on collective farms with the slogan 'If you do not work, neither shall you eat.' According to Dinah, on their return, that had amused her mother no end and the visit had certainly given them much food for thought.

Sir John wrote in his memoir, *The Land Called Me*, published in 1956, 'Their (Russians) belief in the superiority of their scientists over all others was quite touching and I was often asked if I would not like to give up Rothamsted and go to live with them. But on the other hand there was a great streak of terrible cruelty in their character.'

Soon after returning home from such a thought-provoking visit, Dinah had a life-changing meeting. A young man studying at the Aberystwyth College contacted her to ask whether he could borrow her horse to ride one afternoon.

"We kept two or three ponies and I used to hunt – chase foxes along with local doctors and solicitors – people like that. He came and he rode, not very well, and I wondered why he had bothered to come all the way out from Aberystwyth to Glanymor. He admitted afterwards, it wasn't so much the horse, it was me – in fact he didn't like riding!" recalls Dinah.

The romance began immediately, "I was attracted to him too and he came several times after that. He was younger than me but that didn't matter. He had a nice attitude to women."

Stanley Owen Williams was a sea captain's son from Abersoch, North Wales, but within weeks of his birth his father had sailed to the Far East on a three and a half year tour of duty. Stanley didn't really get to know his father until he was seven and he wrote of that memory, 'A Master Mariner's idea of discipline was apt to conflict with my own.'

But when later his father returned from another long tour of duty and Stanley was twelve, he fully appreciated the stories and adventures of a sea captain sailing the high seas and rounding Cape Horn. However, that particular leave had also ended in a great tragedy when Stanley's mother and grandmother died in a house fire.

With his father having to go away on another tour of duty, an aunt offered to look after Stanley. On his thirteenth birthday, he was due to enter HMS Conway Training Ship but a medical examination revealed faulty eyesight and his ambition of going to sea and following in his father's footsteps ended before it began. It was a deep disappointment and when the time came to decide on another career option, after successfully completing his school studies, Stanley was advised that only three were worthy of consideration. In typical Welsh fashion these narrowed down to, 'medical, legal or ministerial.'

Stanley chose medical and was accepted at St.Thomas Medical School, London but during his first year, he suffered another major health problem when he contracted rheumatic fever. He recovered slowly and after weeks recuperating and returning to his studies, he became a patient again, this time suffering from pleurisy. This relapse further weakened him and left him with a heart murmur. It also finished his medical career and he was advised to find a vocation that would involve working in the open air. Stanley faced another set of options and he wrote of those decisions:

'My first love was the sea, my second the land. In the Autumn I entered Aberystwyth University to study Agriculture. I gained a degree but far more important, I gained my life's partner.'

*   *   *   *   *   *

Alas, the course of true love never does run smooth and within months of qualifying, romance had to be put to one side when the outbreak of war in September 1939 gave Stanley further and more serious concerns. He was directed by the University Appointments Board to take an honours course in Chemistry and Agricultural Chemistry. His eyesight and past illnesses had prevented him from joining the armed forces but when he successfully finished the honours course, he was immediately sent to Scotland to do his bit for the war effort as a shift chemist with the Explosives Group of Imperial Chemical Industries (ICI). The factory was based 300 miles away, in Dumfries.

Stanley had proposed and Dinah had accepted but they were facing profound difficulties. Dinah had been aware for sometime that her mother did not approve of Stanley and any talk of an immediate marriage was kept from her. Stanley left for Scotland knowing there would be many direct discussions between mother and daughter, comforted in the knowledge that Dinah had promised to join him. She in turn had come to realise that her mother's objection to the marriage was due, in the main, to her fear that she would be left to farm on her own.

Dinah turned to her brother Sandy for help and he agreed to divide his time between Glanymor farm and his contracting business until a more permanent solution could be found. Bessie meanwhile slowly mellowed becoming reconciled to the relationship and talk of marriage. She and Sandy worked happily together and were able to engage three land girls from the WLA centre in Bow Street to help with milking and general farmwork and they stayed with them until the end of the war. Dinah and Stanley promised they would consider returning to farm when Stanley's work in munitions had finished.

Dinah and Stanley were married on St David's Day, 1st March 1941 at St Michael's Church, Dumfries, the church where Robbie Burns, the great Scottish poet was given a military funeral in 1796. They found good lodgings and an allotment on the site of the Old Rectory and soon they were growing their own food and cycling everywhere. At work Stanley was in charge of 80 female workers and three male foremen making propellant for rifles and machine guns. Their first child, John, was born in Scotland, but although they were living far north, they were not out of range of German planes. A hail of bullets struck the munitions factory roof one dark night when Stanley was inside and the highly combustible chemicals blew up. Luckily Stanley was unhurt but he stayed for hours to assist the firemen to contain the fire becoming cold and wet and as a result, rheumatic fever surfaced again.

"The medicals wanted to take him to an army hospital and they said it was a nine week job to get him back on his feet," Dinah recalls. "No, I told them, I'll cope, I'll look after him myself.

Then they produced a medicine, sodium salycitate and as soon as they'd gone, I poured it down the drain. I had him on his feet in a week. In a fortnight he walked down to the surgery to see the doctor – it happened to be a locum – and he told us, that the medicine he had been prescribed was clearly really good stuff. I didn't let on that Stanley had never taken it, but on the strength of that we had a fortnight's holiday. Stanley realised I was on the right lines. You have to convince them that your own body can heal itself without having to take medication," says Dinah.

"Self-healing is not old wives tales. These are proven practices. His legs were swollen, so I wrapped cold bandages around them and then a warm towel and gradually the swelling went down. Even today, I regularly go to bed with a cold compress covered with a woollen scarf around my kidneys. I have a cold bath every morning, I walk every day. You can look sceptical at me but at 97 I'm well."

Dinah's marriage prompted Bessie to plan her own future and look for a smaller farm. Sandy's business was developing, as was his romantic relationship with a young lady from North Wales and they would soon be married. Bessie realised that Nantllan and Glanymor would not sustain two families and she decided to look around for other tenancies somewhere near the coast. There were holdings available on the Gogerddan Estate four miles to the north, near the sea-side village of Borth. One farm,

Pantydwn had been empty for sometime and needed a great deal of work done but another, Ynys Fergi, closer to the sea was in a better condition and she decided in 1942 to move there while she looked for a more congenial farm.

The village of Borth is built on a drained strip of land between two contrasting features, a four mile stretch of wide sandy beach and sea on the one side with a world heritage site of special interest on the other - the 2,500 hectare raised peat bog, Cors Fochno. Protecting the land from the sea is a high shingle ridge which runs the whole length of the beach guarding the village which seems to cling to its very foundations. The Cambrian railway line runs parallel to the village alongside the quiet flowing River Leri and the bog. Engineers in the 18th century encouraged the river to change its course to become a deep, high banked drainage canal, which begins at Ynys Fergi farm on the south end to flow in a straight line northwards to the Dyfi Estuary. The brown flat expanse of the bog is dotted with several oases of raised land, like small green islands, each one carrying the Welsh name 'Ynys' (island) in its title, and on which early inhabitants squatted to make a living before the Enclosure Act of 1801 played havoc with their land rights.

Family circumstances had obviously now changed since Dinah and Stanley left Cardiganshire for Scotland but after recovering from his illness and enjoying the holiday, Stanley was released from his work in munitions and they returned home to the only available farm tenancy near Borth. Stanley wrote of the move and the difficulties ahead:

'I was released in August 1943 to take over a 300 acre derelict farm. It was on the edge of Borth Bog, far from the madding crowd and was only accessible by foot, horse or tractor. I well remember our first winter there. Mud, gumboots and dishwashing in a bucket on the floor. But in spite of restrictions and shortages, we made a real home there, our first home.'

The farm, Pantydwn, owned by the Pryse family of Gogerddan, was on the edge of the bog, had been empty for years and was a bleak and difficult place to farm. Because of the war, farm productivity was still tightly regulated. The first edict they received from the War Agricultural Executive Committee directed them to plough and plant beans for cattle fodder. The 'War Ags', as these powerful committees were called, were established in every county to supervise agricultural production so that targets such as ploughing up land for arable production and grassland improvement were met. It was a period in which government intervention was of a most intrusive kind, modifying rural landscapes, land use and farming patterns. A few committees took their roles more seriously than others and any tenant farmer who did not comply with orders faced eviction. If you were directed to grow beans, you grew beans, even though the main arable crops grown in Wales were potatoes and wheat.

The number of productive hectares in Wales rose steadily through the next five years, from 215,000 in 1939 to 500,000 at the end of the war. Dinah and Stanley got the buildings and land into some sort of shape during their three year tenure, but Pantydwn was still far from ideal to put down permanent roots.

Within months of their arrival back from Scotland, Sandy married Megan, a sea captain's daughter from Pwllheli and they began their married life farming in Nantllan. Sandy had taken over the milk round from his mother and the contracting business had grown into a flourishing enterprise, most of it due to the 'War Ag' schemes and their targets to plough land for potatoes and arable crops. Tractor power and mechanisation was gathering pace but few small farmers could afford to invest in new machinery to deal with an increase in arable crops, so agricultural contractors were very much in demand.

The majority of farms and small-holdings in the locality were offered as tenancies by the Plas Gogerddan Estate. Since the eleventh century the Pryse family had dominated the social, cultural and political life of the northern part of Cardiganshire and their wealth had accrued greatly in the 19th century from the discovery of lead and other minerals around the Plynlimon hills. The estate prospered and expanded to 20,000 acres but by the beginning of the Second World War, Sir Loveden Pryse, the last of the Gogerddan landowners, was sinking into the abyss of bankruptcy, his estate down to 3,000 acres and unable to invest and improve his land. Many of his tenants too were suffering from a lack of investment and high rents.

The newly formed Farmers Union saw this issue as an opportunity to take action against a landowner who was becoming increasingly forgetful and wayward in his dealings with his tenants. The Union turned to the law and took Sir Loveden to court but it was a lost cause. Instead, in its wisdom, the Court ruled that two of the Union's team, leading tenant farmers, should be turned out of their farms because of their action against an esteemed and influential landowner.

Meanwhile, Dick Jones, who for years had farmed as a Gogerddan tenant at Brynllys, near Borth, a big farm with good quality land, had been embroiled for months in a dispute with the War Agricultural Executive Committee. They had directed him to plough many acres of his land to plant potatoes and wheat, but Dick refused. He had neither the finance nor the implements to comply with such an edict. He was a respected and kindly sheep farmer but elderly, with no intention of changing his system of farming.

There followed a monumental clash of power and victimisation. The Committee led by its chairman, R.L.Jones declared that Dick Jones of Brynllys was not farming his land according to the edicts of government. It was a case for eviction but to add fuel to the fire, the Committee also pointed out that Dick Jones, as a Union man and a tenant farmer had also refused to back the Union's initial allegation against Sir Loveden Pryse. It appeared punitive but such were the machinations of Cardiganshire power politics at their most acute. Whatismore, the son of one of the two deposed tenants from the recent court case, Farmers Union v Lord of the Manor, was also a member of the powerful Cardiganshire War Agricultural Committee.

Dick Jones, the mildest and kindest of men was caught in a 'no-win' situation but he stuck to his principles. He believed Sir Loveden to be an honest and honourable landowner who had treated him with respect and had not raised the rent despite his own serious financial predicament. But the pressure from the Committee was relentless following a statement by Dick in his defence ending with the fateful words, "It is all a matter of loyalty."

Desperation brings out the best in a cornered and desperate 'Cardi.' Dick began formulating a 'grand plan', a wiley solution which he believed would satisfy Sir Loveden and, at the same time, outwit the Committee. He would willingly leave Brynllys – the farm was anyway becoming too big for him – if he could move to a much smaller place on the Gogerddan Estate.

One day out walking the fields and pondering how to proceed with his plan, he met Bessie and when he'd finished reporting the saga, he put a proposition to her.

"You move from Ynys Fergi and take Brynllys and I'll move to the small place. They won't point a finger at you because you've got a good reputation... which I don't seem to have."

Bessie immediately saw the possibilities. Brynllys Farm would be ideal. It was the next farm to Pantydwn and with Dinah and Stanley, they could farm both as one complete unit. It would be an interim measure and would comply with Dick's directive if Bessie could move into the Brynllys house. Sir Loveden, alert enough to see merit in the scheme, agreed and it worked. The 'War Ag' could do nothing but observe while Dick Jones moved to Ynys Fergi, and Bessie left to move to Brynllys.

The situation in late 1943 prevailed until after the war when a Labour government came into power and imposed heavy taxes and death duties on the large land owners of Cardiganshire and they soon began selling their estates. A rural way of life came to an end and the powerful War Ags ceased to exist. It was an opportunity for sitting tenants to buy their leases and become the next generation of landowners. As a final seal on the shift of power, Plas Gogerddan, the ancestral seat of the Pryse family, became the headquarters of the academic research centre, The Welsh Plant Breeding Station.

When legislation was passed and the Gogerddan Estate sold, Stanley and Dinah saw the opportunity to buy the leases of both Pantydwn and Brynllys. Then they sold Pantydwn, their home for five years, to finance Brynllys. The jigsaw was complete in 1948 when Bessie found a nearby farm to her liking, Bryncastell on the outskirts of Bow Street and equidistant between her two children, Dinah and Sandy and their families.

Bessie was very content. At Bryncastell as time moved on, she would welcome her grandchildren, talk to them, teach them and set them to work. She abhorred idleness, so when they visited, they were told to pick up stones from fields, cut thistles, or feed the calves and the work ethic for them too became deeply ingrained. These were now the years when she could pass on *her* colourful stories, knowledge and experience to the third generation. It had been a long and drawn out process but by now she had settled all her children.

Locally Dinah and Stanley had a farm of their own and Sandy was well established in his family home with a thriving business. Bessie could now look forward to enjoying a more leisurely life. Given her character however, she could not give up her agricultural pursuits and so farmed with her customary zeal and continued to give her time to the University as an active member of the Court of Governors.

* * * * * *

The grand plan engineered by Dick Jones plus a little manipulative guile had ensured a stable future for Dinah and Stanley. Brynllys thus became the base for family and farming development into the next millennium. It was over 300 acres of good land, south facing and close to the sea with distinctive old farm buildings of rounded stone gathered from the shore line of Cardigan Bay. The house, well built and solid, needed modernising but it was comfortable for their growing family of three children, John, Elizabeth, Rachel and then baby Dinah born there in 1950.

A constant theme for their mother was the intention to create a truly organic farm using natural systems and methods and Brynllys provided a good base on which to work. Dick Jones had rarely used fertilisers but his grassland needed good management to improve, so Dinah formulated her strategy for the future based on experiences working with her mother at Nantllan. It was to be a mixed farm and the hill rising behind the house would be ideal for sheep but the main emphasis would be milk production from Guernsey cattle, many of them the progeny of the original cattle bought by Bessie in the Reading sale of 1926.

Every cow had been given a name with the prefix of the original parish, Llangorwen, and one particular (if unlikely) name stands out from those years, namely 'Llangorwen Marilyn Monroe', a sexy descendant of the more sedate 'Llangorwen Rose'. Dinah laughs loudly as she recalls, "We named her that because of her wonderful udder. One day Mother went to the solicitor to make her will and said, Sandy can't look after a cow called Marilyn Monroe, Dinah will have her. I think the solicitor thought she'd gone gaga."

Dinah was proposing to establish a pedigree herd of Guernsey cattle and so began the establishment of a long and detailed breeding programme of selection and culling. She much preferred Guernseys to Ayrshires for their excellent temperament and adaptability but it was the quantity and quality of the milk they produced that was their strength. Their milk was naturally high in butterfat, protein and calcium, coupled with a unique ability to pass Beta Carotene, a natural antioxidant, through the cow's digestive system into the milk to give it a rich golden colour.

Selection of a pedigree line is based on past history, temperament and ease of calving, plus the cow's appearance, body conformation, bone frame and udder. Detailed records of milk yields and length of lactation are also important. Past records are invaluable but having a 'good eye', that arcane ability to recognise instantly the qualities that are right for the herd, are vital.

The land at Brynllys drops gently to sea-level and in places to the north west it adjoins the Borth bog, Cors Fochno. There is at once a bleakness and great beauty in the exposed expanse of marshland, with Cardigan Bay to the west and a backdrop of the Plynlimon hills rising gently to the east. In the 19th century many farmers on the high ground supplemented their income by fishing the abundant shoals of herring in the bay, as well as digging peat from the bog in the summer months and allowing it to dry to provide fuel for the winter. Both practices have long since disappeared but living close to the shore was a bonus for Stanley as Dinah had long realised that for him, the call of the sea remained as strong as ever. Farming was not his chosen vocation and he would often say to her, "I could never have farmed without you and Evan, the cowman, with his and your experience and practical knowledge."

Evan was one of seven children who was to stay at Brynllys, a trusted and loyal livestock man, until his death at the age of 90. He was a fount of knowledge on wildlife, farming customs, practices and stories of the past which always seemed more vivid than those of the present. His great delight was football and on Saturday afternoons he would walk from Borth to Aberystwyth to watch Aberystwyth Town Football Club play their home games.

Stanley built a yacht and when John, the eldest son, was old enough, the two would sail across Cardigan Bay to New Quay. Dinah recalls, "He got a lot of enjoyment from that and his lack of real interest in the farm was never a cause for disagreement between us. I understood that, because I loved farming, and he understood my feelings."

Those first years at Brynllys were a real challenge, developing the pedigree herd and improving the grassland. Slowly, Dinah was producing what was becoming a truly, natural, exceptional quality produce. They mechanised the cowshed and dairy, making the twice daily work of milking much lighter and quicker. As she developed the pedigree line Dinah also began taking one or two cows to agricultural shows and regularly they came home as winners.

During this time they rejected all moves to intensify animal production methods in post-war Britain or to add fertilisers to the land in order to produce more. Instead they used many strains of grasses and clovers in seed mixtures for new leys to develop as permanent swards, and also, carefully nurtured the rich mix of plants in old habitats of pastures and meadows.

The majority of farmers were however caught up in the policy of producing more and more from the land by adding a mix of fertilisers, but Dinah was outspoken in her views that commercial pressures were forcing too many changes too quickly. Farmers were constantly encouraged to intensify their production and practices, yet there seemed a lack of understanding of the long term effect, not only on the soil but also on the quality of the product and eventually on animals and humans. Research into the fertility of a dairy herd led by Dr Gareth Williams of the Milk Marketing Board had shown that land fertility went down as the use of manufactured inorganic nitrogen fertiliser went up. There were also other warning signs. There was growing evidence that heavy doses of nitrates, the inorganic source of nitrogen, were poisonous to cattle but the influence of big business plus subsidies to farmers was too great to resist. Consumers, it was argued, were benefiting from cheap food and the farming industry had effective and secure markets for their products.

The term 'organic farming' was not much in evidence in the years immediately after the war and those who spoke against the dangers of intensifying food production were often labelled as 'cranks'. Modern methods, it was argued, brought financial success and kept costs down. Dinah's mother Bessie by now in semi-retirement voiced her opinion in no uncertain manner. "If you want to put British agriculture back on its feet, you want to shoot the agricultural economists. We need to care for the soil, not exploit it. The emphasis on intensive and high density farming can only be destructive in the long term," she said.

Others too were voicing their concerns, notably, Lady Eve Balfour, niece of Arthur Balfour, the former Conservative Prime Minister. She farmed in Suffolk and her career seemed to echo Bessie's. She was the first woman to graduate in Agriculture at

Reading University in 1915. During the first World War she had organised and trained women for the newly established Land Army in England, just as Bessie had in Wales. Both had taken an outspoken stance on natural farming.

Given her position in society, Lady Eve had a wide range of contacts – political, research scientists, nutritionists and many like-minded landowners – and was making her voice heard. She was influenced by the work of Sir Robert McCarrison who had published the results of his research into the relationship between soil, food and health. It was a theme taken up by Sir Albert Howard for more detailed research. This led to a further study, the first of its kind, called the Haughley Experiment in which two farms were compared, one farmed organically and the other farmed what is now termed 'conventionally', using fertilisers. It was the result and conclusion of all these studies that prompted Lady Eve to publish her book, *The Living Soil*, arguing the case for an alternative and more sustainable approach to agriculture.

Her book proved to be the catalyst for a new movement and three years later in 1946, the Soil Association was formed, an organisation that became the heart of organic farming and food, providing the impetus and setting standards for the production of organic products. It was soon after this time that Dinah and Stanley moved to Brynllys to begin their own odyssey into the organic system of farming.

Dinah had been much impressed by the thesis backed up by many years of research expressed in *The Living Soil*. Eve Balfour was a gifted communicator and when she set out her philosophy she began with this thought: *'My subject is food, which concerns everyone; it is health which concerns everyone; it is the soil which concerns everyone – though they may not realize it.'*

In 1952, on one of her speaking tours, Lady Eve Balfour travelled to Wales after visiting the Royal Show at Shrewsbury, where she had addressed a meeting of people interested in organic farming. Sitting in the audience, Dinah was inspired and struck by Lady Balfour's personality and philosophy, and following the formalities of the meeting, she approached her, and immediately made arrangements formally to join the Soil Association. Thus Brynllys became the first certified organic dairy farm in the UK.

Dinah takes up the story. "After that I had a lot to do with her, I liked Lady Balfour because she was practical. She came to stay and we met a number of people. But there were a few youngsters in meetings who argued and gave her a rough time."

Eve Balfour was direct in her talks and lectures around the world, her message simple and to the point – the quality and vitality of soils were fundamental to producing healthy animals and thus human food. In Wales, she could not have found a better or a more effective advocate for the merits of organic farming. Dinah herself began travelling to speak resolutely at meetings and today she reflects on the negative attitudes and the derision she encountered in those days. "You see, our generation was a much harder generation of women. That makes for character. Mother never thought a woman inferior," she paused to emphasise the thought, "and I don't either."

*   *   *   *   *   *

By the early 1950s Dinah and Stanley had expanded their Guernsey herd to 40 milking cows including their breeding programme of around 20 heifers and with a similar number of calves, they averaged about 100 in total. They maintained their policy of out-wintering the dairy cows, who were therefore healthier, cleaner and became better milkers. Many of their neighbours argued that if they kept their cows indoors, they would use less food and produce more milk from their feeding practices because a great deal of food consumed out-wintering would be converted into keeping their bodies warm. But for Dinah and Stanley that argument assumed that the amount of milk produced was directly proportional to the amount of food consumed, but they believed the nutritional relationship and equation was far more complicated than that. Cow A could be producing five gallons a day and Cow B two gallons, although the intake of food was the same. The co-efficient of each individual cow to utilize the food consumed and convert it into milk is acknowledged to be the primary factor, but in calculating those figures, the breeding line and the state of the cow's lactation and health are two more factors to be taken into consideration.

At Brynllys they found their out-wintering policy encouraged the co-efficient favourably in the majority of cows in their dairy herd. Calf rearing was another important aspect in the production of healthy cattle and their method at Brynllys was different from the majority of farmers. Dinah firmly believed that to maintain good health, a calf should receive wholemilk direct from the cow and for that reason, they designated 'nurse cows' from the milking herd. Four calves would suckle each cow for about 16 weeks and their intake would be in the region of eight and ten pounds of milk a day. In her opinion, the cows and the calves looked healthy and contented. It was costly but they believed the calves not only thrived and in the long term paid the best dividends. At that time, in the early 1950s, milking between 30 and 40 cows, their annual milk production was around 35,000 gallons (155,000 litres).

In addition to Guernsey cattle, they also kept a flock of Clun Forest ewes, a hardy and adaptable breed of sheep plus over 100 hill sheep over winter, 300 hens, two breeding sows, and 60 weaners bought in for fattening. It was a truly mixed farm with feed from organically grown grazing leys with the right proportion of leafy grass and white clovers to maximise protein content. Additional crops included kale, oats and peas, and a small acreage of mangolds and cow cabbage. Oats were an important and widely grown cereal crop in West Wales and because of oat adaptability to the soils and climate, it was most suited to meet the needs of livestock farms. The oat straw, also useful for bedding, was slightly unpalatable but its feeding value was infinitely superior to wheat straw and slightly better than barley. Oat grain was also an important ingredient for producing superior quality milk as the form of starch in the grain was especially suited to the digestion of farm animals, so the overall dual-purpose nature of the crop gave it an added value.

In many respects Dinah and Stanley were self-sufficient, especially growing their own crops as fodder. Fields were set aside to make hay for winter feed but often hay-making was a race against time in the coastal climate, with a need for at least four sunny days in succession to allow the leafy grass to be cut, turned and dried in full bloom. It was difficult making good quality hay at Brynllys and they found before the days of big bales, that raking dried grass into very large mounds – much larger than the traditional method - maintained the quality and nutritional value without much deterioration. That was not always possible when the dark rain clouds loomed over Brynllys to interrupt the hay-making process, but eventually an investment in a barn dryer solved their summer problems. In fact the hay quality was so good, that milk production increased by 200 gallons per cow per year.

Bessie and Abel in 1908

Crugiau Farm, their first home

Abel Jones with members of the UCW Aberystwyth Dairy Department

Mrs. B. L. Jones, Nantllan, Clarach, Bow Street, Cardiganshire, writes:— " The Early Potatoes which you had photographed were grown with your Special Early Potato Fertiliser. I was very pleased with their progress and lifted 5 tons per acre at the beginning of June. I hope to use your manure again next year."

Early potato growing at Nantllan, Clarach Valley

Bessie Jones's milk delivery cart led by 'Bess', the family horse

'Granny' Bessie Jones at Bryncastell Farm in 1958

DAIRY SHOW CHAMPION.

Dinah Jones, aged twelve, of
Aberystwyth, winner in the milking
contest for boys and girls under
eighteen at the Dairy Show.
[Alfieri.

Dinah aged 12 in 1923

Dinah, winner of Talybont Races on her beloved horse 'Tory' at Nantllan

Dinah and Stanley's wedding on March 1st 1942

Dinah winning the Production Inspection Cup, Cardiganshire
National Milk Records in 1966 against all breeds

The 1982 snowstorm that blocked access to Brynllys for two weeks

Margaret and Shan making Rachel's Dairy yogurts at Brynllys in 1984

Rachel's Dairy first design in 1984 by Jim Goodband

John delivers yogurts in 1985

The view north over Brynllys Farm to the Dyfi Estuary

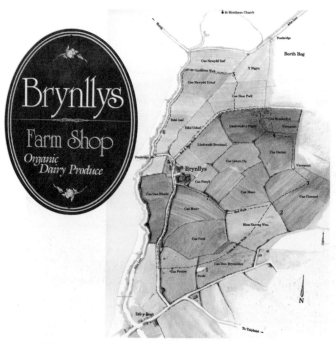

Map of Brynllys fields showing the walks open to the public, 1988

Rachel in the Brynllys farm shop selling produce in 1988

The Rowlands family, 1991
(John, Mark, Rachel, Dinah Williams, Shan, Gareth and grandson Llyr)

Gareth and Rachel in 1987

Rachel with Brynllys Champion
Guernsey at the Royal Welsh
Agricultural Show, 1991

John Rowlands competing at the Horse of the Year Show in 1982

Dinah celebrating her 80th Birthday in 1991

Rachel and Dinah in 2004

Llyr at 18 months enjoying his grandmother's yogurt!

Tasting Rachel's new flavour products at home in 2005
with Shan, Jo Tett (Technical Manager) and nephew Rhys

Rachel receiving her MBE at Buckingham Palace in 1997

Rachel shows HM The Queen around the dairy section
of the Royal Welsh Show 2004

HRH The Prince of Wales tours Rachel's Dairy in 1998

Dinah and The Prince discuss family associations with the Glamis Estate.
*Inset picture: Dinah's grandfather William Brown (centre) meeting the
Earl of Strathmore, the Prince's great-grandfather*

Original Rachel's Dairy pot 1984   Rachel's Dairy pots 1987

Rachel's dramatic new black pot 1998

New bilingual Welsh butter 2001

The UK's first branded milk 2002

Rachel's is officially designated a 'Cool Brand' in 2007

Against this backdrop though, slowly Stanley's health was deteriorating. The illnesses of his early years had weakened him and physically he was not robust enough to cope with heavy manual work in all kinds of weather, winter and summer. By now they also had four children, three girls and one boy. John the eldest, Elizabeth, Rachel and the last born, Dinah, named after her Welsh Mam-gu and her mother.

The children and her marriage brought Dinah deep happiness. "My husband was a tolerant man and a peacemaker," she remembers fondly. "Being confrontational gets you nowhere, although you have to have some individuality in order to survive in a good marriage. The farm, the business and our marriage were a real partnership for us."

Following much discussion, they both agreed that Stanley should relinquish working on the farm and use his knowledge and experience of animal husbandry in a consultancy role. Eventually he took a post with the Ministry of Agriculture Livestock Advisory Service at Mold, North Wales. It was not an easy decision as it would take him away from his family Monday to Friday but he loathed being idle and, more important, a regular salary meant he could maintain his contribution to their overall income and play his part in their future security. So began his weekly working routine, leaving Dinah to run the farm.

These were difficult years as the 1960s dawned. John the eldest boy was about to begin a degree course in Agriculture at Edinburgh and within three years he graduated to return to the farming enterprise at Brynllys. But like his Scottish great-grandfather and uncle Sandy, his real interest and delight were not in animals but in machinery. The natural farmer of the family was his sister Rachel, who had a deep and sympathetic understanding of animal husbandry, especially dairy cattle. Dinah had spotted a real talent in her and even at a young age she had great commitment.

Stanley had settled into his new routine, leaving on Monday morning and returning on Friday with John taking more responsibility for the farm. It was time to look to the future and the generational hand-over. Stanley began looking around for a suitable small-holding in North East Wales so that he and Dinah could be together and also for Dinah to maintain her interest in farming. He wanted Dinah to face the reality of their future together and how best to give the next generation, John, an opportunity to farm Brynllys. He would maintain his work with the Ministry and have an independent source of revenue. It would seem to be the best solution for everyone.

There were protracted thoughts and discussions, punctuated suddenly by the death of Bessie in July 1963, aged 84. It was hard to come to terms with the fact that such a resolute and remarkable woman was no longer there as head of the family to guide them and be their mentor. Always proud of her Scottish ancestry, Bessie had put down deep roots in the Cardiganshire soil and had contributed handsomely to the agricultural industry and the community. Many tributes came from far and wide but none was more appreciated than the letter sent by Bessie's old friend, Sir John Russell, long since retired, and living in Oxford. He wrote to Dinah:

'It was a wonderful life, and she was a remarkable woman, achieving much in face of difficulties which never seemed to daunt her. Never can I forget the impression she made when she first came to Aber. We had never seen anyone quite like her. And when troubles came upon her, we marvelled at the way she faced them and by strength of character overcame them. She was a mother to be proud of and she can never be forgotten by those who were privileged to know her.'

Bessie had enriched her Welsh family. She had bucked the trends and chose to do what she did because she believed in it. She was quite capable with her intellect and experience to argue against any detractors.

One of the hymns she chose for her funeral shortly before she died was 'The Sands of Time.' Written with a frail hand, she issued the instruction, 'Number 581 in the Scottish Hymn Book' – she never forgot her roots – a hymn that was well chosen.

For Bessie was perhaps one of very few women in agriculture to leave such a large footprint in the sands of time.

*   *   *   *   *

Whilst Dinah and Stanley had arrived at a decision about their own future, it was becoming obvious that John, their son was not finding farm work easy or satisfying. Dinah was helping as much as she thought wise but he was struggling.

They turned to Rachel, the more natural farmer and invited her and her new husband, Gareth, at the time living near Bracknell, to farm Brynllys in partnership with John and his wife, Morag. Initially they could live together in the house until a new house could be built on the land. It was 1966. No one believed it would be easy but it turned out to be a period of extreme difficulty. Different personalities and different attitudes clashed, and the schisms that occurred at that time are still keenly felt today more than 40 years on.

It was going to be almost impossible to run a farm successfully under the circumstances, but within months Dinah suffered another agonising blow. Stanley died suddenly and she was left to mourn a man who had been the rock in her life for 25 years. If anyone could have negotiated a peace deal in family disagreements it was Stanley, but it was not to be. Now there was uncertainty about her own future and that of the farm.

"It was hard," says Dinah. "I carried on because mother had carried on. Her marriage lasted 17 years and mine 25." Her comment is followed by a long, painful, memory-filled pause.

The difficulties and disagreements within the partnership continued for a further two years until the accountant, trying to make sense of the financial situation, eventually said to Dinah, "You will have to sort this out and only you can do it. Bring everyone with you.'

By all accounts everyone was aware that it was a make or break day. Was Brynllys farm to die or to prosper? Would the family disagreements be resolved or would the partnership split?

Finally it was Dinah's decision, face to face with everyone. With her customary resolve and courage, she faced the problem firmly and positively. The partnership had not worked and was unlikely to work in the future. By the end of the day, Dinah had made her choice. The present arrangement would cease and she would actively involve herself again in Brynllys farming affairs in partnership with Rachel and Gareth. No-one left the room until everyone had looked at every detail and agreed the package.

Now there was to be no turning back, although it must have caused such heartache for Dinah, as she and Stanley had worked so hard to make the farm a viable financial enterprise. Dinah had developed a successful pedigree herd and when it came to the crunch, she had chosen Rachel, not John, her eldest child and her only son, to take the farm enterprise forward as an organic livestock breeder. Harsh decisions are often necessary when families run businesses. Loyalties and relationships can take precedence over objective business arrangements but in this case, Dinah combined her professional acumen with her understanding and love for her family. Ultimately it was also important that the future of Brynllys as a certified organic dairy farm should continue and prosper. It was a seminal moment in the family's times and history and it had been contentious and difficult. Dinah's leadership, foresight, fairness and resolution had ensured stability for the future.

The prosperity of the Brynllys farming enterprise depended on the quality of their produce. The herd of pedigree Guernsey cattle was central to the success of the business. It had steadily increased in numbers and a careful breeding programme had ensured its development and quality. Dinah's reputation was by now widely recognised. Almost every year her Guernseys won prizes and championships at major agricultural shows. She had become a respected cattle judge and was an active member of the Soil Association and of the local Grassland Society. "I've been on all sorts of committees, Milk Records, A.I. and so on – the whole kaboosh. I'd say my piece and often they would laugh at me. Why? Well I was a woman. But I never let them get away with it," she recalls.

In reality, the achievements of her contribution to pedigree livestock breeding were widely acknowledged in her appointment to the Welsh Agricultural A.I. Panel where detailed discussions on the merits of bulls and progeny are discussed and measured. It is through the work of this panel that the quality of Welsh livestock is maintained for the future and Dinah's knowledge and experience is highly valued. She remains a life-long member of the Grassland Society, rarely missing a meeting and her challenging remarks still keep farmers half her age on their toes.

After Stanley died she also became active in other spheres and her involvement and achievements were recognised when she was appointed Fellow of the Royal Agricultural Society, one of the very few women to receive the honour. She became an activist in the National Farmers Union and later was appointed Chairman of the Ceredigion NFU county branch. She was always keen for women to play a more active role in the union's activities so there could be balance in discussions. As to her political affiliations, she says, "Oh Mother (Bessie) was always a Conservative. They used to say, if you weren't Labour at 18, you hadn't got a heart. If you were not a Conservative by the time you were 40, you hadn't got a head. My father had always been a Liberal, but like my mother, I became a Conservative at 40."

Perhaps Dinah's greatest contribution has been her leadership and passion for organic farming and her inspiration to others interested in its principles. She was a pioneering member of the Soil Association and was instrumental in the establishment of its West Wales branch. Their first meeting was held at Brynllys Farm and to this day she regularly attends local and national meetings voicing her concerns at every opportunity.

She would host gatherings for groups of people and use the farm to demonstrate livestock husbandry of how to combine effective cropping, rotational grazing with natural habitats. Often she was invited to visit small-holdings to encourage and give advice to new people who had moved to the countryside to live 'the goodlife'. She was always deeply concerned, and still is, that many such people didn't understand how to make their dream work and lacked the principles of good agricultural practices. Often she would leave a 'lifestyle' farm shaking her head.

"They'd tell me, it's wonderful we've come back to nature, but what people have to understand is, you don't control nature, you work with it. Maybe their hearts were in the right place, in the heavens probably, but it's not real. Also if the aesthetics of your surroundings are untidy, the mind can also be untidy."

Reality for Dinah was working and understanding the land, making a commitment and a financial input. Otherwise it is a hand to mouth existence or failure. She believes firmly that in farming you have to leave the land in better heart than when you inherit it and for that you have to work hard and be disciplined. During conversations, often punctuated with laughter, Dinah recalls a full life, of incident and challenge with constant references to her mother's influence in so many ways. Dinah had enormous respect and regard for Bessie's achievements and her legacy. When asked of her own achievements, she says, "I've always worked hard. If there were problems, they were resolved. Nothing was insurmountable. I had an affinity with farm animals and I sometimes think of Evan our old farmhand as he too had that affinity with them. He said to me once when I asked him what he missed from the old days when he was a young man at the turn of the 20th Century. He said it was the rhythm and sound of cutting pasture with a scythe. I thought that it was so evocative, the rhythm of an older time and a way of life."

At a moving occasion at the Royal Welsh Agricultural Show in 2008 at Builth Wells, Dinah was celebrating her 97th birthday. Surrounded by her family and friends she attended a luncheon in honour of those who had sponsored different aspects of the show. Fine weather had ensured a happy four day show and as the Chairman of the RWAS Council, Alun Evans, concluded his short speech, he announced to the 200 plus guests that Dinah Williams was celebrating a notable birthday. He invited the President, Trebor Edwards, well-known farmer and singer to lead the traditional birthday greetings in song. The sound almost lifted the marquee like a gigantic hot air balloon, such was the warmth of feeling for one of the Society's most revered Fellows.

In her lifetime, Dinah has created her own legacy and like her mother before her, did so against much of the 'conventional' wisdom of the past 60 years. As a result, Brynllys has become a beacon for the organic system of agriculture that future generations of her family can enjoy.

"You see, my relationship with Rachel when she took over the farm, has simply been as mother and daughter. And that's how it was with mother and me. I knew Rachel was a farmer with commitment. I hope I've been supportive. I think I have."

*   *   *   *   *

RACHEL

RACHEL

"All I wanted to do was farm," says Rachel, her tone of voice quiet and determined, a ring of familiarity to the statement. Like her mother and grandmother, Rachel's intention for her future was apparent at a very young age.

"I wanted to leave school and be part of the farm and that's what I did at 16, after O levels. Now, I just wonder, was I right?" she ponders.

Today doubts surface when she recalls that decision she took as a teenager.

"You see the trouble is, my grasp of the English language is inadequate. I struggle and get frustrated because I can't explain myself in a constructive way, especially at meetings and committees. And then I feel inferior."

An unexpected and surprising statement given that Rachel's name has become synonymous with success. She is the third generation of women in a family who, for decades in the 20th century, has carried the torch for organic farming. What is more, in the last 20 years, together with her husband Gareth, she has created a company which has grown to be one of the leading organic food processing companies in the UK. She has eloquently argued the cause of organic food production against all negative attitudes, pressures and prejudices and, in the last decade, seen the market for organics grow significantly. In the tradition of her mother and grandmother, Rachel is uncompromising when it comes to extolling the nutritious merits of organic food products and how to achieve a sustainable and profitable system of farming, without bending to commercial pressures. Rachel thus has little reason to feel inferior.

On a bright sunny day in the conservatory at Brynllys, Rachel's mother Dinah (now 97) appears, her face wreathed in smiles as bright as the morning sun. The close bond between them is clear. There is mutual respect and the conversations range over past achievements and disappointments, memories of family life, relationships and business concerns, the future of farming and rural community life. Both recall with affection the stoicism and ground rules set by the strong personality of 'Bessie Brown from Scotland.'

From the conservatory at Brynllys there is a panoramic view of much of the farm to the west. Beyond a small copse there is the sweep of Cardigan Bay; to the north west the expanse of the raised peat bog, Cors Fochno and then the two long lines of dwellings that make up the village of Borth built on a strip of land between the sea and the bog. Beyond the last house there are the undulating sand dunes that lead to Ynyslas and the wide Dyfi Estuary. To the north, behind the house, a hill rises gently to 500 feet. Pastures, hedgerows and trees are preparing for Autumn, their work done following a hot summer, the green leaves giving way to pale browns and yellows. A flock of sheep grazes quietly on the slopes but there is no sign of the prestigious Guernsey pedigree dairy herd. They were sold five years ago when Rachel and Gareth decided to hand over the reins to their daughter Shan and her family. The next generation, the fourth in the line of women, is again reshaping the future of the farm.

Brynllys was modernised a few years ago into a comfortable spacious farmhouse. The large kitchen with a double oven Aga is the hub for affairs of the day where Rachel prepares food and often entertains. It opens into the newly furnished conservatory on the south side and a door on the other leads to a hallway and an office where all the farm's administrative affairs are dealt with and stored. Everywhere is light and airy. There is an overwhelming impression is of colour, comfort, warmth and tidiness with everything in its place.

Brynllys is reached from the main road through the pretty village of Dolybont and, as you turn into a narrow lane that bends after half a mile, the farm appears as a mixture of old and modern farm buildings. Large barns and sheds meld with the light grey, solid stone walls of the original buildings which were once a cowshed, calf pens and the dairy. They are all well kept, not a slate or stone seems to have moved with the passage of time and those walls which have been rendered with whitewash gleam in the sun. Hedges have been carefully managed to thicken growth and provide shelter for wildlife and livestock. There is an unnatural silence in the yard, as though the milking and dairy buildings are resting after years of hectic activity to store their memories in blocks of stone.

Brynllys may no longer be involved with dairy cattle but it remains resolutely organically farmed and that means a positive attitude to the environment. The two go hand in hand. In recent years there has been frustration within the farming community as to environmental policies and dictats introduced by different government agencies. Often they are seen as inflexible, with not enough consideration being given to tried and tested farming practices. Rigid protocols for cutting hedges or ploughing certain fields by particular dates often see the environment in isolation from agriculture and the farmers who tend the land. While policy makers seem to lack understanding of how farming and nature work together, cheap imports, supermarket buying practices, food scares and government regulations have turned a once thriving viable British agriculture into an industry in crisis. The experience Rachel has inherited as a practical farmer, establishing a successful organic dairy processing business, as well as contributing to organisations and agencies involved in food production, have given her a rare insight into the problems of the future of modern agriculture.

When the business was fully established some 25 years ago, the name Rachel's Dairy became synonymous with natural milk products of the highest quality. Flavours, textures and tastes were based on Granny Jones's original recipes and the principles of dealing successfully with milk without additives. Putting the emphasis on developing a breeding programme for the Guernsey herd was then paramount and in the early years Brynllys relied heavily on Dinah with her keen eye and deep knowledge of livestock. That experience and wise counsel has been passed from generation to generation but Granny Jones, Dinah and Rachel would be the first to agree they would not have achieved their goals without the input of their respective partners, Abel, Stanley and Gareth.

There have been difficult, low times compensated by highs and many joys and personal fulfilment. "There have been disagreements within each marriage," says Rachel, "But they have never been restrictive because the men of the family recognised their women as equals and in many instances, they have been the driving force in setting the agenda for the chosen system of farming."

Rachel and Gareth have been in partnership for over 40 years, and during one conversation Gareth made this observation, "I'm often perceived as 'Mr Rachel'! I'm proud of that, and now I'm extremely proud that our daughter Shan has stepped in. She told us, it's important to her that Brynllys remains organic. So now we're into the fourth generation of women here."

Rachel and Gareth met when they were both gaining practical experience and training at Llanllyr, the home farm of the Hext Lewes Estate at Talsarn, in the wide Aeron Valley inland from Cardigan Bay. Rachel had completed one term of an agricultural course and Gareth, ironically intent on changing direction, had applied for a post as a trainee with the chemical giant ICI at a subsidiary research centre. Gareth and Rachel were attracted to each other and fell in love, but within weeks he heard that his application had been successful and almost immediately left for his new life. Within a short time, Rachel realised with certainty she was pregnant. The reaction from parents was understanding and a wedding was arranged, at which point, it seemed, a career in farming was no longer a viable option for Rachel. She left the college course and her family to set up home with Gareth at Bracknell where the ICI headquarters was based.

They began their married life living in a mobile home near Ascot. Gareth was 21, Rachel 18. Living in a strange urban environment could have been daunting but, newly married and in love, Rachel made the most of her time by becoming a homemaker. Her situation was similar to that of her mother when she set up home in Scotland. As she looks back on her early years, Rachel acknowledges that she was influenced by her mother's nurturing and disciplines. It is hard to believe today when she recalls the dichotomy within her own character. "I was not an easy child, always being inquisitive and questioning and yet wanting to comply and please," she says.

Curiosity and the joy of being married made her determined to settle into her new life and surroundings. She explored the countryside around Ascot walking three miles to the town to shop for provisions, noting on her walks all the subtle changes in the fields and woods. They had little money and budgeting for all their needs was a real challenge but the family's Scottish and 'Cardi' traits of thriftiness saw them through. Gareth's work often took him away to Somerset where ICI were conducting trials on new weedkillers at their Home Farm. It was a well paid job with good career prospects and like all new employees, he was allocated shares in the company, working a 37.5 hours split shift (5-9.30am and 5-8.30pm). When his boss remarked that he had not submitted claims for payment of his overtime hours, Gareth answered in his typical direct manner.

"I'm off all day. I have a car. I have an expense account. I can behave like a tourist and visit places in Somerset and Dorset. I'm having a wonderful time."

During the first months of the marriage, Gareth suffered from bouts of very high temperatures as a result of having contracted Undulant Fever from his contact with Brucellosis infected cattle at Llanllyr. When antibiotics failed to cure him, he eventually took Rachel's advice and submitted to the Naturopath method of body cleansing and healing. A series of cold compresses around the kidney area helped cleanse and purify his system of the toxins causing the disease. As a result Gareth had first hand experience of Rachel's family belief in the ability of the human body to cure itself.

Although focused ironically on non-organic agricultural products, the training at ICI was well spent, learning the principles of running a successful business, managing people and the importance of keeping accurate accounts and being financial accountable. Gareth was on a three month stint in Somerset when their first child, Mark was born. With the days of waiting now over, Rachel suddenly became busy as a full-time mother.

When Dinah and Stanley came to see their new grandson soon after the birth, the conversation one night turned naturally to news of Brynllys and during that pivotal visit, they first raised the possibility of Rachel and Gareth returning to farm. The thought and hope stayed with Rachel, but Gareth was engrossed and enjoying his training. A few months later, the idea turned into a firm invitation from her parents to return to Brynllys to farm in partnership with Rachel's brother and his wife, John and Morag.

For some time Rachel had realised that her brother John was struggling, not least because his heart was more in machinery than in livestock and crops. Rachel would have said 'yes' immediately - she would be returning to her roots - but there were more serious considerations. Gareth was carving out a successful career in a well paid job that had a measure of security. He vividly recalled his mixed feelings at the time.

"I was enjoying myself. But, as I gave the proposal serious thought, turning over the pros and cons, the 'buts' became stronger. There is a hankering in the Welsh. If they leave Wales, they've got to come back. On the other hand, the idea of farming, of being involved in a new enterprise was great, although I didn't understand a great deal about it, and I didn't understand how the family worked."

Gareth is a proud Welsh countryman born and brought up in Tywyn, a seaside town to the north of the Dyfi Estuary. His father was in charge of the local abattoir at a time when all animals for slaughter had to comply with Ministry rules and be graded for quality. Although not directly involved with farming, the influence of the main industry in the area – breeding sheep and beef cattle, plus tourism – was the basis of growing local prosperity. Gareth's experience of the milk industry was limited but he knew Rachel was steeped in dairy herds, milk production and organic farming, and he could bring his business experience to the enterprise. He also had to embrace organics.

Following many discussions into all aspects of the proposal, how to share responsibilities, who did what in the family deal, there was a heightened expectation as they analysed the legal and financial aspects of a partnership. Many of these issues were resolved with Dinah and Stanley acting as arbiters so it was with great excitement and hope that Rachel and Gareth finally agreed to come home.

Once there, they set about obtaining planning permission to build a bungalow for themselves close by. Initially the two families shared the house but that was often difficult. Two young families needed space, and tensions were unavoidable as they waited for completion of the new place. Occasionally irritations would erupt into full blown rows, more especially between John and Gareth, both strong characters. Rachel was caught in a disagreeable situation of familial disputes between her brother and her husband within months of setting up the partnership. She could understand both their personalities and sympathised with John's attitude.

As a boy he had set his heart on becoming a sailor like his grandfather but John, as his father Stanley before him, never fulfilled that ambition because of an accident when he was eleven years old. John had joined two sons of the family living in their old home, Pantydwn out in fields and woodland shooting pidgeons when suddenly, John received a direct hit at close range.

The sequence of events leading to the accident is unclear but John received a shot to his arm leaving it severely damaged, hanging limply, a mangled mess and twisted. He spent the next two years going back and forth to the Orthopaedic Hospital at Gobowen in North Wales undergoing operations to repair the damage, but his hand and arm had become withered and weak. He was thirteen when he resumed his education at the grammar school at Aberystwyth but he never lost sight of his dream of joining the Naval Academy, HMS Conway on the shores of the Menai Straits on Anglesey. He was interviewed for a place three times, the last following an appeal, and eventually he was accepted. That experience had a profound impact on his life. His initial joy was tempered when, a little while later, he faced the reality of the rigours of a seaman's life, and a realisation that he could never become an active sailor.

Rachel acknowledges his dilemma. "It must have been hell for him coming to terms with the accident and how it changed the course of his life."

Management of the farm was becoming a major problem and however hard Rachel's father, Stanley, acted as peacemaker, the disputes continued. Gareth was not by nature a compromiser. As Rachel comments, he saw most disputes in black and white. However, and as time passed, when Rachel and Gareth moved into their new bungalow, the tensions eased but it had been an uncomfortable period.

Stanley's sudden death in 1966 rocked them all. He had been at the centre of the development of Brynllys, a well-loved husband and father and a wise and respected head of the family.

Of his father-in-law, Gareth says, "I had lost someone I could work with and respect. I could talk and exchange ideas with him. Stanley had vision. He was a particular kind of Welshman and very much a peacemaker."

It was an immense loss at a time when the young people taking over needed his counsel and leadership. But the hard decision of how to deal with disputes and the long term future of the farm was left to Dinah, and she did so with her customary stoicism and realism.

Two years later she made her choice and took her decision in front of her children. The much hoped for partnership was not working and Rachel and Gareth were chosen to take the farm forward. It was difficult for Rachel. She felt the loss of her father keenly and the anguish of acknowledging a failed partnership with her brother called for self-control and resilience.

Gareth remembers that day vividly, when, in the surroundings of a formal office they were all gathered around the table and the accountant outlined the package for the future. "Oh, I felt for my mother-in-law. She had been through so much. It was a huge day," he recalls.

The schism had caused much heartache. Relationships could have fractured completely but everyone at that gathering faced the reality of the situation openly and honestly by recognising personal limitations and priorities.

$$* \quad * \quad * \quad * \quad * \quad *$$

Thus Rachel and Gareth began their farming challenge in 1968, at a time when conventional farmers were being asked to be ever more commercial in attitude and intensive in practice. Such folk were earning more money than ever before. Regular payments through a fixed pricing structure for products such as milk and potatoes, in addition to subsidies, gave the impression to the public at large that farmers were feather bedded. Some went so far as to call it the 'Golden Decade,' but there were others who forecast long-term disaster.

The American author Rachel Carson had published her warning on the dangers of intensive farming in her book, *Silent Spring*. Agriculture had become a high input industry using massive amounts of fertilisers, water and pesticides. Farmers throughout the world began adopting newly developed crop varieties bred to increase yields, such as wheat with shorter straws to support larger heads of grain without toppling over and making harvesting easier. Yet as the 1970s drew to a close, the good times faltered. Spiralling costs of food, outbreaks of foot and mouth disease and fowl pest, concerns about farm safety, misuse of chemicals, and even the weather seemed to get worse.

Against this background, Rachel and Gareth fared reasonably well. As organic farmers they were not in the business of intensifying production for profit. Gareth, who had embraced the organic ethos, had realised that organic principles and respect for the soil were far more important than the quest to produce ever more. This was not the time to compromise those principles and they began to formulate a plan of action.

They were efficient and productive at Brynllys but their future needed further investment if they were to prosper. They needed to acquire more land to increase the number of dairy cattle. More dairy cattle meant more buildings. It would be a risk because money was tight, the children were growing up and, as Gareth remembers, "Everybody was working very hard but there was not a lot of money in the system." But they accepted the challenges and like many others, new buildings, bank loans and development plans became part and parcel of their lives.

Meanwhile, over-production in the subsidised agricultural industry soon led to stock-piling of products with warehouses filled with European butter mountains and milk lakes. Surplus dairy products which seemed lucrative on paper, in reality, once produced, were impossible to sell. By 1975 there were over 500,000 tons of unwanted European butter waiting to be sold for next to nothing. Then came a beef mountain, several varieties of grain mountains, and surprisingly, a wine lake, all as a direct result of the European Common Agricultural Policy (CAP). One correspondent observed at the time, 'A harvest of bureaucratic brilliance and interventionism gone awry.'

Established in the 1960s, the Common Agricultural Policy (CAP) is a system of European Union agricultural subsidies and programs. Until 1992 the agriculture expenditure of the European Union represented nearly 49% of the EU's budget. The CAP combines a direct subsidy payment for crops and land cultivated with price support mechanisms, including guaranteed minimum prices and subsidies. At an EU level, it led to huge imbalances in supplies of primary agriculture produce, resulting in the need to apply quotas to individual farms.

Originally the CAP had been established with ambitious goals to achieve agricultural self-sufficiency, stable food prices and an improvement in living conditions for farmers. When Europe began producing surpluses, the CAP propped up the industry by buying and storing the excess produce giving rise to the lakes and mountains. Subsequent reforms only managed to curb the worst excesses, and in the process, came edicts which only added layer upon layer of complex grants and subsidies. Such was the increase in form filling that it was a wonder farmers had any time to grow anything!

By the early 1980s, there had been considerable investment at Brynllys. They had increased the Guernsey herd to 55 milking cows mostly bred from their own stock. Dinah's experience and knowledge in cattle breeding helped Rachel to develop her own style and judgement in selecting and maintaining the right type of cow. In the past they had selected a bull of a certain type to keep on the farm, but they also relied on the choice available from the Artificial Insemination (AI) service.

In summer time, Gareth and Rachel would often be seen parading one or two cows in Guernsey classes at agricultural shows, occasionally winning rosettes but always dreaming of the day they would win the Supreme Championship at the main event, the Royal Welsh Agricultural Show.

They had more success in England when one of their pedigree bulls won the Supreme Championship at the Reading Guernsey sale and this seemed to compensate Dinah for her failure all those years earlier. As time passed and experience deepened, the dairy farming community recognised and acknowledged the quality of the Brynllys dairy herd based on Dinah's knowledge and judgement.

Many farmers in Wales had similar ideas on investments and expansion such as building milking parlours and making milk production more efficient. On the other hand CAP had begun to focus on the possibility of introducing milk quotas that would limit the production of milk on every dairy farm in the European community. The discussion and debate was prolonged and difficult in the CAP corridors of power. There were rumblings of immense anger within the farming fraternity, especially from the dairy producers of West Wales.

By now Rachel and Gareth had a growing family – Mark, John and Shan. Their futures would soon be important, but how could Brynllys sustain the next generation if production was to be restricted by milk quotas? However before the CAP quota proposals became a reality, fate intervened at Brynllys forcing Rachel and Gareth to act on an idea they had often thought about and discussed, namely farm diversification.

*   *   *   *   *   *

A major snow storm which proved to be one of the most severe of the 20th century hit West and South Wales on 7th January 1982. Rachel recalls the day. "It was a Friday. Mid-morning. Gareth was looking out of the window and he said, "I think we'd better do something with the sheep."

It was close to lambing and they set about coaxing the pregnant ewes into the barns from one of the bottom fields. "It took us all day, because sheep are so silly in the snow. They want to go on their own paths and to their own places," explains Rachel.

The blizzard coupled with strong easterly winds blew the snow into 20ft high drifts which continued throughout the day and night, some 36 hours in all. When the sheep were safely coralled, Gareth and Rachel turned to milking with the winds howling and blowing snowdrifts into the cowshed. "We shovelled in turns as we milked and the children got involved too. But the weather forecasts were ominous."

Rachel kept a diary of those days and the urgency and tensions of looking after animals in trying conditions comes through in her writing and daily entries.

Friday 8th January. *'Lane blocked by lunchtime. Bull pens full of snow. Had to move them to another yard at the back. Old cowshed full of snow and calf pens covered. Cows had to be milked in the top part of the shed only. Impossible to walk facing into the wind. Snow freezing on my glasses. Bitterly cold.'*

The following morning the wind continued to blow strongly. Although it had stopped snowing, a white blanket covered the land and the lane was impassable with drifts as high as the hedges. It was impossible to move anywhere. Thankfully the regular Milk Marketing Board tanker had collected milk on Friday morning but it was very doubtful that a collection would be possible during the weekend. The ground had frozen solid and there was little sign of a thaw, so they faced the problem of storing the 450 litres of milk produced each day.

"Gareth heard the gloomy weather forecast and determined as ever, decided to act," recalls Rachel. "He telephoned his friend Ianto who had a JCB, but it was kept in a yard eight miles away. They decided to walk to the Capel Bangor yard and from there attempt to open up the road and the lane."

The walk took four hours. However, they retrieved the digger and managed to get through the drifts but it was slow and difficult progress. Darkness fell and when they arrived at Llandre, a village a mile and a half from Brynllys, the digger broke down – or it may have run out of fuel – but suddenly it stopped and flatly refused to budge. It was now 10 o'clock, pitch black and Gareth decided to make for home. Taking a short cut through a nearby caravan park, he slipped on ice and badly broke his ankle but somehow managed to crawl painfully through the ice and snow to a neighbour's house.

Rachel had gone to bed, not unduly worried because she knew the task of clearing the lanes would take a long time and she had to get up early the following morning to milk and feed the stock. A telephone call from Gareth told her what had happened and because it was impossible for an ambulance to get through, he said the neighbour would try and take him to the hospital in the tractor box to the nearest point where the main road to Aberystwyth had been opened. It was a cold, painful, bumpy ride as an ambulance met them and took Gareth to hospital.

The diary for the next day, begins with the dramatic heading in capitals:

Saturday 9th January. *'GARETH HAS BROKEN HIS ANKLE. Still bitterly cold and strong wind. All of us up to tackle the milking. Prepared the dairy to begin making cream. Bulk tank practically full. Terrible night for Gareth.'*

"I felt for him – the pain, the anguish, the anger and the frustration, but there was little I could do. All I could say was don't worry, the children are here, we'll cope," says Rachel.

And cope they did. The outside yard resembled a winter wonderland ice-rink. Milking 45 cows in a cowshed that had 35 ties and stands was normally a simple procedure, but changing cows already milked with those waiting their turn, all of them uncertain and frightened on the slippery surface became a nightmare. So was carrying hay and feed from barn to yard, to pen and cowshed plus feeding sheep in the fields. Every water pipe in the outside system was frozen solid.

Reflecting on the scene, Rachel recalls, "We couldn't wash udders, and there was no drinking water for the cows. We had to defrost what we could before we could begin. The children were terrific. Shan at 13 ran the house and prepared meals, and the boys, Mark and John worked outside. Sam, the full-time worker, walked from his home in Borth and stayed here a week and an apprentice walked two miles from Bow Street and stayed two weeks."

It soon became obvious that milk held in the bulk tank would not be collected for days and after milking on Saturday night, it was already full. Early Sunday morning Rachel made a decision. "We are going to separate the milk. We have the old electric separator. The skim milk can go to the cows, they'll drink that instead of water. We'll store the cream and I'll try and do something with it later on."

Monday, 11th January. *'Very hard frost. Pipes frozen. Neville walks to work and stays the week. Margaret calls to offer help. Very pleased to see her. Washed cream containers. Children home from school. Sam and Elfed opened up the hedge in the bottom meadow. Dilwyn to town to fetch cake and sugar-beet, unloaded onto trailer the other side of the river. Jack and Eirwen take me in to see Gareth.'*

Not a drop was to be wasted. The apparatus and old fashioned implements for making dairy products, such as the separator and butter churn, had been carefully kept after Granny Jones's death. Meanwhile they searched out and used every clean container in the house and on the farm, but as Rachel observes, "When you start separating milk, you need to be vigilant about cleanliness.

The separator is full of parts and they have to be thoroughly washed and cleaned again and again. So with little water we had our work cut out but in the end we didn't waste the milk, we didn't throw it down the drain, - that's what kept me going."

There were no further snowfalls but the strong wind continued to blow snow in swirling clouds from the fields, depositing it around the hedges on the lane, turning the white blanket into a patchwork of stark winter colours, the dark green of the fields, the black tips of the hedges bordering a white stripe which marked the lane. Tractors and 4x4s were much in evidence and to gain access to the main road, they opened gaps in two hedges before they could cross the River Leri to reach the road. A week after the snow-storm, the main road was eventually cleared and the milk tanker at last got through to the nearby village Borth. They had been milking twice a day and carrying supplies of milk across the fields to people without milk in the village. Storage was becoming critical but Rachel had managed to extend her area of activity by asking her cousin, who had a four wheel drive, to help her take pots of cream to shops and hotels in Aberystwyth using the gap in the hedge in the bottom meadow as an access point.

Borth became the central point for milk collection for all dairy farmers in the district and it remained so for six days until the farm lanes were eventually cleared. To everyone's relief, it was also the day Gareth came home by ambulance from hospital.

The storm had proved costly for most local dairy farmers. The majority had poured thousands of gallons of milk away and sheep farmers had lost hundreds of lamb bearing ewes in drifts and the bitterly cold weather. Estimates of those huge losses in Wales reached £2.5m.

Yet, the incidental home-produced products at Brynllys had sold well and Rachel received many compliments on the quality and taste of her cream. The surplus cream she had churned into butter. Such was the interest that people asked her to continue the service on a regular basis. Rachel was not geared up for such an undertaking but the idea provided much food for thought and discussion. In very few weeks, the Rowlands had decided to regularise their commitment to retail cream in the locality. However the facilities were basic, using many of Granny Jones's old implements in a small stone whitewashed dairy opposite the house.

They began deliveries and in the first year, from Easter 1982, Rachel separated about 4,000 litres of milk out of a total farm production of 240,000 litres. The second year they more than doubled the output to 9,000 litres. It was the beginning of their policy to diversify the farm's productivity and add value to their milk. They also began employing a few local people to help in the production process and distribution.

During that period there was mounting concern about the proposal by CAP to introduce milk quotas for the dairy industry. The concern turned to anger when they heard the announcement that the policy would become a reality in April 1984. The most vocal and notorious public protest in Wales was staged when the then Minister of Agriculture, Michael Joplin, visited the Llangadog creamery in Carmarthenshire. He was virtually imprisoned in his car while a crowd of protesters turned the taps of milk tankers to release thousands of litres to create a river of milk. The fierceness of their protest was a reflection of the deep feeling in west Wales, where farmers for a decade and more had been encouraged to expand production, borrowing from banks to invest heavily in new machinery and buildings in order to increase efficiency. The majority were small family farmers for whom milk production had been the only source of income, so the imposition of restrictive and limiting quotas, introduced almost overnight, meant they could not easily increase production and would face financial difficulty repaying debts. Any long term farming plans or developments were immediately stifled.

The quota scheme was introduced two years after Rachel had begun retailing cream and a little butter. The quota for Brynllys meant they would be capped to produce a quota of just 240,000 litres of milk.

"For a farm this size (254 acres) that was a low figure because the calculated value of the milk on an annual basis was a gross income of £39,000. The gross value of the milk (9,000 litres) we had turned into cream was £9000 during the previous year of retailing. It didn't take much to work out what the potential of our annual milk production could be if we turned our total milk output into cream. £250,000 would bring the opportunity to generate a higher profit and a far better opportunity for the farm to sustain itself," explains Rachel.

The opportunities were clear but they were at a crossroad and there were vexing questions to be answered. The boys were growing up. Mark was 15, and both he and John were interested in being involved, but there remained the question as to whether the farm could generate enough income to sustain a family of five. There were significant risks and their deliberations intensified. Central to all these issues was the quota forcibly allocated to them based on their past production figures as a mixed organic farm. It seemed like a penalty.

They argued for an increase to 300,000 litres. Gareth and Rachel had already worked out a development plan to achieve the increase in output but it was turned down. The negative answers and attitude were frustrating because they knew that a farm of comparable size, farmed intensively in the 'conventional', non organic way, would have received double that and a quota of 600,000 litres.

Brynllys was a mixed organic farm with sheep, pigs and store cattle in addition to the dairy herd, so they were allocated a certain acreage to grow concentrate feed for their livestock, summer and winter. A conventional farm would be pumping fertilisers on grass and crops in order to increase output and, in addition, they would be buying in concentrate feed for the winter. Farming organically does not allow intensive production practices but encourages animal welfare and promotes bio-diversity. When quotas were being allocated, the Rowlands seemed to be penalised on that score too.

"It was so limiting on our aspirations. We appealed again without success, but around that time we recognised a key loophole in the CAP regulations. If you turned milk into wholemilk yogurt, the milk we produced would remain outside the quota system," says Rachel.

As it happens, for sometime Rachel had been experimenting with yogurt making in her kitchen using instructions and recipes she had found in old dairy books and Granny Jones's notebooks. Initially she used skimmed milk left over from making cream and which she previously fed to the pigs. When she was satisfied with the quality, taste and nutritious content of the product and that she could sustain the quality on a regular basis, they decided to go into production at Brynllys. The decision to produce fresh organic yogurt was based on Rachel's belief that customers appreciated natural goodness and, given the choice, consumers would be willing to pay extra for quality. With good quality Guernsey milk they were convinced that they could create a premium for an organic yogurt in competition with cheaper and aggressively marketed products.

It was a major turning point and a leap of faith that thus saw the tentative beginning of the company and in the three years between 1984 and 1987 they generated sales of between 70,000 and 80,000 litres of yogurt. Eventually the authorities also increased their milk quota. Winning the appeal served as a driving force to generate financial investment and gave them confidence for the future. It was the impetus they needed to expand the farm. They increased to 70 milking cows and quickly found new markets for the extra products.

Rachel's inspiration and guiding principle for yogurt production stemmed from Lady Eve Balfour's philosophy in her book *The Living Soil* where she states, 'We measure food production in terms of yield or quantity per unit area, but the real measure is not more quantity but the total human health value of the crop produced.'

"I passionately believe our food is crucial to our well being. Purity and integrity should be the by-words for the food we sell to our customers under the organic banner," says Rachel.

In finessing her recipes, Rachel researched the history and methods used by ancient civilisations to produce fermented yogurt from natural milk. For commercial production, the only difference today is that milk must be pasteurised before it is given time to ferment.

"It was hugely important and advantageous at that time that we had a Guernsey herd," says Rachel. "I don't know that we would ever have infiltrated the market if we hadn't had Guernseys. The quality of Guernsey milk gave us a superior natural product. I experimented a great deal in those early days. I knew that after taste, the most important quality was to generate the smooth mouth feel, a yogurt with some resistance and a thickness to it."

In the beginning, the yogurt making facilities at Brynllys were quite primitive given the sensitive task of controlling temperatures over periods of time. Containers wrapped in blankets were placed in the airing cupboard. An old freezer cabinet was used to control and maintain the temperature. Bowls of hot water generated heat and were placed at the bottom of a metal chest and containers of yogurt were put on a shelf at the top. The lid remained closed overnight to maintain a constant temperature until the yogurt had set. The following morning the containers were placed in a cold water tank to drop the temperature before putting them into a chiller. It was basic but it worked – and, of course, at all times Granny Jones's principles of strict hygiene were always observed!

The first delivery van was basic too. They lined it with double duvets to keep the pots chilled and maintain a constant temperature for eight hours, at least for the time it took to complete the delivery round. "We were always conscious of health and safety regulations. We regularly invited trading standards and environmental health officers here to inspect our production methods, such as they were, and if they could identify practices not up to scratch, they were corrected immediately. In fact we pre-empted those problems – remembering again how hygiene and cleanliness had been drilled into me by Granny Jones. As for packaging and branding, in the early days I wrote simple labels and stuck them on the sides of plain plastic pots."

In 1986, they analysed their business results and looked to the future. 38% of sales were to shops and service units, 20% through local distributors and 42% through regional distributors. Things were going well.

Thoughts of expansion had surfaced early on with their first achievable goal being to use all the milk they produced by increasing yogurt production. They had proved that although there was a strong client base in West Wales, they needed an aggressive marketing policy and more sophisticated branding to expand the market geographically by targeting potential distributors and larger populations further afield in the West Midlands and the Thames Valley.

Ideas for expansion were examined in detail before they were satisfied they could go ahead. Gareth believed in expansion but he felt they needed to collect more information on finance, logistics, productivity and market trends and examine the figures thoroughly before making a commitment. The business should expand at its own pace. Rachel, perhaps a more instinctive person, had great faith in the consumer who she believed would recognise quality and a natural product. Gareth needed the evidence, while Rachel believed they should capture the moment and expand immediately. They both recognised the risks they faced, especially the financial ones, and when they had completed their analysis, they decided to move forward.

Rachel reflects, "It was my belief in the consumer that drove me. I felt we could process on a large scale. Gareth too had the will to do it. It was a leap of faith for both of us but little did we realise that we were actually pioneering Britain's first organic dairy brand!"

The same spirit of adventure, of risk taking, of being an entrepreneur that had sustained her mother and grandmother were clearly also driving Rachel. As with them too, it was combined with resolute determination and hard work.

*　　*　　*　　*　　*

Finding the right identity for the product, an appealing name and image to attract new customers was the first and most pressing task. During their first years when they were selling locally they were content to use, Brynllys, the farm name. But they had begun talking of building a purpose built, off-farm production unit and a new name and logo were imperative. In 1984 they invited a group of friends involved in organic farming and retailing to share ideas and discuss possibilities. They sat round the table following a good supper tossing names, titles, metaphors, descriptions – 'Yogurts of Brynllys', 'Guernsey Yogurt' etc, when Peter Seggar, a local organic farmer, suddenly said, "Why don't you call it Rachel's, or even Rachel's Dairy?"

It was inspired. At once, so simple and so right. The ultimate seal of approval came from Gareth who, with an eye to the future said, "That's great, because our daughter Shan, is called Rachel Shan and so it can involve her too."

They set about commissioning designs for their yogurt pots and their first brand image. Looking back, the word 'organic' did not feature in the title, nor was it included in the descriptive strap-line or any other graphic material simply because at that time, the public did not fully understand the full implication of the word. Ironically, although organic was important to them as producers, the Rowlands did not see it as an effective marketing feature.

Initially, they simply saw their product very much as local food for local people, everything else was a bonus.

But as the public became aware of the significance of the word organic, their next change of identity included a succinct explanation of the organic movement. Part of the remit in those early days was to educate the public and convey the meaning of the word 'organic' and Rachel spent many hours at food fairs explaining its merits and qualities of the product to shoppers.
The concept of 'live' yogurt was also difficult to explain. On one occasion a customer peered into the pot demanding to see what was live and why was it not moving!

Confidence in marketing techniques grew when Rachel attended a six week course by Mid Wales Development for those who wished to set up businesses.

"I knew how to milk a cow and turn it into yogurt, but I hadn't a clue how to draw up a business plan or a marketing strategy," she says.

When she completed the course, attending one day a week for six weeks, Rachel was allocated a mentor who followed their business activities for a year and helped guide them through the process of setting out a marketing plan.

"It was really helpful. Attending the lectures during the six weeks I would say to myself, well yes, 'we're doing this' and 'we're already doing that' etc. So we must have been doing much of the marketing work instinctively, but it really did give me confidence in the way I talked to people. My life up until then had been raising children, the family and working on the farm without much contact with the outside world. Suddenly, I had to go out and persuade people to buy the product! How on earth could I do that?"

At the time, there was thus a tendency to dub the organic system, 'alternative' or 'fashionable farming' but Rachel and Gareth were adamant that, as their business grew, it was not alternative farming and not deviant. It was traditional and how farming should be done. One interview for television from those early days stands out in her mind. The knowledgable presenter and farmer, Dan Cherrington, of the BBC television series 'Farming' visited Brynllys. He was a genial man, but sceptical of the new business venture, especially one dealing with an organic product at a time when organic products were not fully accepted by farmers or the public. When he arrived, Rachel was milking the cows, the perfect background to the interview and without a second thought, he pointed the microphone at her to ask pointedly, "But how are you going to sell your product?" Her reply was equally pointed, "Oh, I'll tell them what it is and that I'm so proud of it and what a lovely product it is."

When she saw herself on the screen, Rachel was taken aback. "It just came out like that. It's the belief I showed, and on reflection that is exactly what helped me, that strong belief in the product and having the understanding of why we do things the way we do. Also having the confidence and the ability to deliver it."

It was the natural quality of the product that was uppermost in her mind, and in the early years, using the same recipe, she would try different cultures and fruits in order to find different ways of improving the consistency or thickness of yogurt. One day she was explaining her intention to a culture salesman who had called at the farm to discuss her production method. He suggested that by adding one or two additives, the problem could be easily solved.

"I was amazed, completely taken aback. I'm only going to produce what is going to be good for my customers," she told him, "I don't want to be adding anything. I'm not in the business of additives. I'm only interested in the quality of the ingredients and the end product. It has got to be natural quality for health."

Today Rachel's sustained enthusiasm and fervour on the subject is based on her knowledge of the development of food processing and manufacturing during the past 50 years. Her belief in organic food is unequivocal. Health is affected by the quality of food we consume and the nutritional value of that food is vitally affected by the way in which it is grown and subsequently processed.

"We farmers produce food but manufacturing companies have made vast profits at the expense of consumers and the health of the nation by what they then do with it. Ready-made meals, additives, colourings and excessive salt have influenced the taste of natural products. Understanding nutrition and feeding ourselves well have not been important issues. Today we are reaping the effect of those practices. There are big problems of national health and welfare, although there are at last attempts to turn the clock back to create better awareness of natural quality food," she says.

In parallel with all the changes and growth that took place in 1987 - the business expansion, the new logo and new marketing techniques - the Rowlands also opened Brynllys Farm to the public. There were farm trails, talks on systems of farming and caring for the environment, a farm shop, regular demonstrations so that visitors could recognise how the various processes of milk production and organic farming went hand in hand with conservation. They created walks of different lengths to view pools and weirs, amenity tree planting, hedgerow and herb-rich pasture management, all designed to give pleasure and allow people time to imbue the Rowlands' passion for nature.

It was all part of Gareth and Rachel's initial mission to explain organics and create an awareness of how the organic system was helping sustain the environment. They passionately believed organic farming did not function in isolation from the environment or the community and that it must be in sympathy with natural habitats. They listened to comments from visitors and were amazed and frightened at the lack of understanding of farming and food production. Twenty years later, much of that has still not changed and according to Rachel, it begs the question why the teaching of food production and domestic science has virtually disappeared from the school curriculum.

Communication was an important aspect of their early success. Direct contact with people at functions and fairs, one-to-one conversations followed by articles in general interest and women magazines began getting the message across. But distribution of supplies and reaching the right markets in populated areas posed a worry and as a company, they were constantly attempting to expand their client base and breakthrough to the big retailing businesses.

Meanwhile, the local Trading Officer, a regular visitor who kept a close eye on the quality of their products and the standard of their production methods could occasionally throw an odd spanner in the works. He arrived unexpectedly one morning in 1984 to scrutinise the process in the dairy when they had just taken delivery of 50,000 pots. Immediately his attention focused on the layout of the information and the graphics on the pots. There were different coloured lids to denote different fruit flavours. That was incorrect he told them. All the information regarding the content should be on the side of the pot so that it was easily visible to the customer on what he maintained was 'one panel vision.' Rachel and Gareth maintained their cool and patience, pointing out that the batch of 50,000 pots had just been delivered and they simply could not make changes immediately. A quick calculation of their current sales figures meant that it would take a year to clear that particular batch. In reality it took nine months. Thankfully he was a kindly Trading Officer able to exercise his own judgement and a particular brand of leniency, but the incident was a salutary lesson in the minefield of food regulation.

It is difficult to comprehend how Rachel could accomplish all the tasks she faced every day, being a mother with a growing family, running the home, cooking meals - often taking bread out of the oven at midnight, getting up at five to milk, plus making and marketing yogurt, cream and butter.

"The whole thing was growing very fast but in truth, I had more pleasure in receiving letters from satisfied customers who wrote the words 'thank you' than I did from any income we generated," recalls Rachel.

*   *   *   *   *   *

Wighin four years they realised that thoughts of moving out of the farm dairy at Brynllys into bigger premises had reached a critical point. By now, there was a growing consumer awareness and demand for organic foods and, as their output at Brynllys increased, so the need to streamline and modernise their production methods became more and more apparent. Three factors dominated their deliberations before they could be satisfied that they were ready to face making a huge financial investment to build new premises. Above all they had reached the limit of yogurt and cream production at Brynllys. But to expand further, they would also need a supply of organic milk from other sources to increase output. A few farmers in the area had already turned to organic production but Gareth and Rachel would need to look to other areas of Wales if they were to increase their supply of milk. Furthermore, their marketing would have to be much more sophisticated and aggressive to ensure their product would be stocked regularly on supermarket shelves. Finally, they needed to be confident and prepared to bear the risk of borrowing a vast amount of money to build, equip and staff a new purpose-built plant.

Gareth recalls those days. "When we went into the dairy challenge, there was a lot of naivety on our part. But it was at the right time in the development of organic products and we had the good sense to move with it. Also, there were a lot of people out there who had a lot of experience who could come and help us – and they did."

From the beginning of the venture, Gareth had undertaken the administrative and accounting side, leaving Rachel free to develop and execute production. He and Rachel were a team, complementing each other as they searched for solutions to problems and working toward the same goal. Gareth was a proud Welshman, passionate about its language, culture, countryside and inevitably, rugby. Rachel was passionate about farming, food and health. They were in partnership, self employed, investing and expanding a high risk business which at times was exhausting and put emotional strains on their relationship.

The move off farm and expansion called for unwavering confidence and once the decision had been taken, there followed months and months of planning, obtaining a site, encouraging other farmers, budgeting, setting targets, visiting possible sales outlets, marketing and PR and above all, selecting and training staff.

The most complex aspect of all was the new dairy plant itself, its construction and the new equipment required to maintain the quality and texture of the final product. With no personal experience of commercial manufacturing, they relied much on designers, consultants and experts, briefing them with figures on the proposed input of milk and the production output they hoped to achieve.

"We made mistakes, of course we did. We said to ourselves in those early days, if ever we do this again, we'll be so much wiser! Relying on experts is all very well, but identifying those dependable experts is another matter. It was a huge step," says Gareth.

The economic development support agencies in Wales bent over backwards to find ways of assisting although at times it was not easy, especially dealing with those who had the authority to apportion grants. Commercial scale food processing was a comparatively new business undertaking in Wales and amongst the many and varied regulations to qualify for a grant was that all the stainless steel equipment should be brand new. Nothing could be second hand. As Rachel puts it, "It all seemed illogical, because stainless steel equipment is stainless steel equipment, new or second hand. As thrifty farmers, we would instinctively have looked for a more economic, pragmatic solution."

They received support from the Mid Wales Development (later the Development Board for Rural Wales), a government agency that assisted businesses and prospective employers in the region. The Board agreed to put up a factory building on the Glanyrafon Industrial Estate on the outskirts of Aberystwyth and to lease it to the company for a reasonable rent, but the Government's Welsh Office (in the days before the Welsh Assembly Government) refused their application for a grant.

"It was frustrating and a bitter disappointment. But twenty years ago, I suppose they didn't have faith in us or in our product. We didn't have that track record," says Gareth.

Another particular concern for Rachel as they headed toward expansion concerned the issue of processing milk from other organic dairy farms, five in all, two in Pembrokeshire, one in Oswestry, and two in Ceredigion. Organic milk was collected separately from those farms and transported and administrated by Milk Marque, the wholesale company that had replaced the Milk Marketing Board. The real challenge for Rachel was to maintain the authenticity, taste, and nutritional benefit of the final product, because it was likely the constituent values of milk from other herds would be inferior to Guernsey milk. Rachel was determined that the final quality should not be compromised.

Milk for processing needed a consistent minimum protein level of 3.8% and 4% of butter fat to attain the quality consumers demanded from Rachel's organic yogurt. But the level of protein in much of the milk from other suppliers was generally lower than that figure, in part due to the different breeds of dairy cattle, but also due to the seasonal variations and richness of grazing. To achieve the figure of 3.8% protein, moisture had to be removed by evaporation, which meant a significant energy cost coupled with the added investment of installing an evaporator. Achieving the right level of protein following evaporation increased the percentage of solids in the milk and concentrated the flavour. The new suppliers agreed to regular testing procedures and to concentrate on the nutritious mix and value of feed given to their cattle, not least because milk flavour is also dependent on the quality of grazing and fodder fed to cattle.

Taste was another dimension. Rachel had also tried other techniques such as osmosis, to reduce moisture content, but the taste did not have the same profile because a proportion of lactose, another important component was removed during the process. Also, removing lactose did not give the microbes so much to work on during the fermenting process with the result that the yogurt left a much drier taste. The whole process of testing and tasting using the new equipment took a long time before Rachel could be satisfied with the consistency of the output.

The thirteen staff she had employed at the Brynllys dairy moved to work in the new plant. They were the basis of a work force well aware of the strict rules of cleanliness and other guidelines and possessing the necessary qualities and standards to produce a high quality product.

As they planned the new dairy, the Rowlands looked to establish new markets, initially in small shops and medium sized health food shops but the real break-through came when Sainsbury's, their first UK supermarket, became interested. Rachel had met a director from Sainsbury's whilst serving on a food award judging panel and she took the opportunity to raise the possibility of selling Rachel's Dairy organic yogurt through the supermarket chain. It was a fortuitous and effective conversation and she soon received a letter from Michael Morgan, Director of Sainsbury's dairy products department, who wrote, *'We have talked at some length about organic products in our business and you stress that your products are at least as good and probably better than most other organic products (such as yogurts) on the market today. If this is so, and we will obviously do some more testing, then I am sure we would look sympathetically at introducing your product into some of our supermarkets.'*

Rachel remembers the impact the letter had on them. "Our approach and persistence had paid off at a time when supermarkets were looking to develop organics and also, their slowly developing policy of supporting smaller regional producers. It was a terrific boost."

In many ways this was the impetus and encouragement Rachel and Gareth needed to crystallise their ambitions and move from the farm to a purpose-built production unit on the industrial estate at Aberystwyth.

"The first day I went to the new plant to begin the production process was the first day that I left home to go to work," recalls Rachel. "I remember when it was first built. It was like a hollow shed. Then it became a huge state of the art stainless steel dairy and we wondered whether we would ever fill it! The first week, in May 1992, we processed 5,000 litres of milk; six months later we were up to 15,000 litres and when we sold the business seven years later, it was 60,000 litres a week. Today it has increased threefold, to 180,000 litres processed into 225,000 kilos of yogurt a week."

The new dairy was unprepossessing outside but inside, gleamed with shiny new equipment of tanks and pipes, packaging and pallets, plus cold storage areas ready to deal with thousands of litres of milk. Increased production also brought other issues such as the complex legislation governing food processing and distribution, plus many pressing aspects to consider in a developing company - from logistics to plant machinery, packaging to refrigeration, sell-by dates to customer complaints, as well as managing the workforce and creating new products.

"At times it was utterly exhausting – trouble shooting, juggling different demands and of course, financing an evergrowing business, knowing our farm was on the line should we fail," says Gareth.

Asked about complaints or critical comments Rachel said, "Fortunately there were not many, but there were some. People who wrote to claim they were ill after eating the product. It's very rare to be ill from yogurt but it was important to acknowledge and reply. In the same manner we dealt with complaints about taste, but that's very much a subjective, personal matter."

The dairy building on the Glanyrafon Industrial Estate was officially opened in September 1992 by the then Secretary of State of Wales, the Rt. Hon. David Hunt MP with a 20 strong workforce. It had the capacity to process three million litres of milk a year and the growth of production at the beginning was steady rather than spectacular. The Sainsbury's agreement gave the company the sales injection it needed, but the main volume product was organic yogurt bearing the Sainsbury's own brand. "We had to tread a fine line between sales of the supermarket own-brand and building up our own brand and market position," explains Rachel.

Initially, as a trial, Sainsbury's had agreed to stock Rachel's Dairy brand yogurts in 30 stores in the South West Region. The success of those sales led Sainsbury's to ask them to produce Sainsbury's own brand organic wholemilk yogurts with the promise of supplying 200 stores throughout the UK. There followed some hard negotiations because Gareth saw the dangers in becoming a commodity supplier at the expense of building the Rachel's Dairy brand.

The Sainsbury's senior buyer, Paul Barber, who understood their production methods and aspirations, was sympathetic. Gareth takes up the story, "People like Paul were key to the business at certain stages. I said, look, we need the opportunity to grow and you've got to give us that opportunity to put our own Rachel's Dairy brand on your shelves. We can't be doing things just for you because it's the Sainsbury's policy. But there was little give on his part in the early stages. The truth was, we needed the volume output and the money because we were so much in debt. But crucially at that stage, as a sign of faith and goodwill, he made an increased offer of £250k worth of business. We took it of course and continued with the Sainsbury's branding but we did a further deal and the Rachel's Dairy brand organic yogurts were eventually stocked in 120 Sainsbury's stores as well. The same yogurts - Natural, Strawberry and Apricot sold alongside each other and it was interesting and gratifying to see that often the Rachel's brand outsold Sainsbury's own!"

These were critical times in the development of Rachel's Dairy, but from the outset they had to run two businesses side by side, both the farm itself and the new processing plant. Mark, their eldest son, young and inexperienced in many respects, had taken on the day to day running of Brynllys. He was now milking 70 cows, but fortunately they had a wise mentor as experienced back up. As Gareth recalls, his mother-in-law Dinah had eased off work at the age of 81 but was now back in the thick of things.

"Dinah was tremendous. She had to move back into the farm. Someone had to walk the farm on a daily basis. She may not have liked what she saw, but when it was seen, it was dealt with until one of us came home. And there's always been that kind of involvement. It's been that kind of relationship at every stage. We were all working hard and she has always encouraged us to move on. We were lucky to have someone of Dinah's experience on hand."

From the very early days of retailing, Rachel had been experimenting with fruits and flavours in the Brynllys kitchen. She developed her own recipes for organic purées and jams and only when she was satisfied with the colour, consistency and flavour were they introduced into the yogurt. During the time they were operating from the farm dairy, a young housewife and mother from Taliesin, a nearby village would make the jams, but when they moved to the new plant, the operation became too big for farm kitchens. They tried to identify companies who could make jams to their specification.

"We could never get the right flavour profile from them. They added flavours, colours and thickeners and the moment we discovered some of those practices, we knew we couldn't engage them, so we decided to make it on site," explains Rachel.

They looked at a wide range of equipment but in the end resorted to an old-fashioned, very labour intensive Heath Robinson affair that worked best. Over the years, manufacturers and processors had carefully developed an enhanced sweet profile for yogurt but

Rachel insisted that their product must be free of additives. It was to be natural and simple. "It was fruit, sugar and yogurt, that was all that was in it. I'd go to the factory sometimes and smell apricots and strawberry jams being made in simple vats and you'd think flavours would be lost, but not so. No matter how far technology has moved forward, the old methods maintain the flavour best."

Making yogurt - in small amounts in farm kitchens or in tons in mechanised plants - the process remained unchanged and constant. But as the company grew there were many changes to the image especially to labelling and colour. Marketing techniques and branding never stand still and soon, following the official opening there were other changes. In order to describe their product accurately they used the words 'Pure and Natural' displayed in bold graphics on all pots to create a better understanding of the true meaning of organics.

"When we put pots with those words on supermarket shelves, sales went up – dramatically," recalls Rachel. "It was a valuable lesson."

Customer reaction was all important, such as an early letter received from Weston-Super-Mare.

I am not normally given to writing to food producers either with praise or blame, but in this case, I wanted to write to commend

*your yogurt, which is far and away the nicest and creamiest I
have tried so far. I think I have been through virtually the whole
market of natural yogurts. It also satisfies certain other personal
criteria namely that it contains no gelatine and that it is a product
of our own shores – previously the best yogurts I tasted were
imported from Germany.'*

However, the increase in sales brought other concerns. Not least,
they were constrained by the shortage of organic milk produced
from Welsh farms and thus the ability to expand their output fast
enough to cope with demand. "Perhaps the hardest lesson in
business is learning to manage growth effectively," reflects
Rachel. "The first two years were particularly hard. Debts were
mounting and the dairy was not able to generate enough money
to cope with interest rates and the demands of high capital
investment. Gareth carried a lot of the financial responsibility
and when the company was under pressure, he kept those
concerns to himself because he was also conscious that we could
lose the farm. In fairness he never buckled. Looking back now, I
realize the pressure he was under."

Producing and processing a perishable product calls for rigorous
controls and from the outset, through all the development and
expansion, appointing and training staff was high on the agenda.
In the early 1990s however, there were very few suitable training
courses available locally for food processing businesses. Rachel

was left to design her own and relied on core principles, her own experience and intuitive grasp of training needs. Conscious of the fact that she did not have an academic education, she found the work of setting out structures, principles, protocols and tick boxes extremely challenging. Working from instinct she knew the basic tenets needed for a training programme and at the earliest opportunity, she appointed Joanna Tett who had recently graduated in food technology. It was important that anyone involved in training should have a complete understanding of the problems of handling milk products and a thorough knowledge of processing technology. It was to be a complete programme of courses for different aspects of the business at different stages in the process. Training courses were not merely targeted for specific tasks but took into account that many new staff coming into the company would benefit from other, more general human development courses. Today Joanna is still with the company as Technical Manager.

In five years they had come through some of the worst aspects of development and investment and by 1997, the supply of milk matched demand. Sales had increased, and the Rachel's Dairy brand of organic yogurt was doing well in Sainsbury's supermarkets and other major retailers were also interested. As they looked forward to the new millennium, Gareth and Rachel began discussing the possibility of creating a new image for the product prompted by John, their second son, who had been involved in the business from the beginning. He was now the company's General Manager and believed it to be the right time to have a general review because branding and advertising techniques were changing rapidly and the original Rachel's Dairy branding was beginning to look dated.

Rachel and Gareth went away on holiday to relax, but thoughts of new plans for new projects were never far from their minds. Away from the day-to-day pressures of the farm and the business, they were able to analyse objectively the direction the company should take. Was change necessary and or should they continue in much the same way? Rachel was adamant that the process and quality of the product should not be compromised, that taste and authenticity remained as important as it was when they first began production on the farm, but they both agreed that it was the right time to modernise the image. A few general calculations estimated the investment they would need for designs and market research, and by the end of the relaxing break they had decided to go ahead. The holiday had stimulated change and they set about revamping their yogurt pots, investing in design that would display a new confidence and underline their position as pioneers in organics.

Eventually they chose a radical and dramatic approach in the form of a black pot. Rachel remembers the particular, decisive moment they opted for change.

"When they put a black pot on the table, we just looked at it, almost in silence. I wanted to pick it up, handle it, turn it around and around in my hand. It really looked good, different and stylish."

Gareth was characteristically forthright in his reaction. "Black! You can't have black in a dairy cabinet." Then he picked it up, turned the black pot around slowly in his hand. "Yes, yes, it did indeed look good," he recalls. The concept was new, bold and exciting and for Rachel it conveyed a sense of daring to be different.

But the ultimate test would be the market place and a foray into market research for the Rowlands. The local supermarket, Safeway, allowed them to place pots of the new designs next to each other on the dairy shelves alongside the existing Rachel's Dairy range. When consumers came into the store, walking through the avenues of shelves to the dairy section Rachel and Gareth watched as their eyes were immediately drawn favourably to the black pot. At that point they knew it was right.

As Rachel comments, "Black reflected quality. And that's what organic is about – quality. Picking it up was the first point. You know if people want to buy your product they must want to pick it up. Next it has got to taste good – we had worked long and hard on that of course. But that's how you maintain sales.

Anybody can buy first time, but repeat sales are the key to success. Quality has been our mantra and at all times, quality control has been central to our production policy."

The new branding was not merely about colour but was also about words and graphics. The immediate visual impact of both was crucial, the core message 'Pure and Natural' remained, and the reverse side of the pot stated simply:

'Made with bio-active cultures and organic skim milk. Our natural yogurt is set in the pot to give a fixed smooth consistency and balanced flavour. Rachel's Dairy yogurt is produced in harmony with the environment. Organic food production is a modern, sustainable system using less of the earth's resources.'

That was the message on the outside of the stylish new pots. Inside was quality organic yogurt, the product of 15 long years of hard work and enterprise.

*   *   *   *   *   *

Having committed to the new dairy the Rowlands family realised very quickly that business never stands still. You either move backwards or forwards and with rapidly increasing sales and ever changing regulations, Rachel's was moving forwards very fast indeed. Soon it was time to extend the production facilities and by summer 1997, along with new machinery, a new cold store and loading bay had been installed at a cost of another £300,000. The plant could now handle some five million litres of milk and accommodate refrigerated supermarket lorries. Gareth was quick to strike a unique deal with supermarket giant Safeway. Their Aberystwyth store was the last port of call for their Midlands run and Gareth managed to persuade them to stop their empty lorries en route back and take full loads of Rachel's yogurts, thereby reducing overall food miles and transport costs.

The new extension had been built with help from the Welsh Development Agency and the then Secretary for State for Wales, Ron Davies MP had been invited to officially open the development. A slate plaque was commissioned and a VIP reception planned for Monday 1 September 1997. Staff worked all weekend on the site including erecting and dressing a marquee. However on the Sunday came the tragic and dramatic news of the death of Diana, Princess of Wales in Paris. All official Government engagements were cancelled and the Cabinet recalled to London as the nation reeled in shock. In Aberystwyth, the marquee was quietly dismantled.

However, by a strange twist of fate, the following year, the dairy was to receive a visit from HRH The Prince of Wales, a keen advocate and supporter of organic farming. The previous year's plans were resurrected and with a different slate plaque, the new extension was finally officially opened.

By now, the company had grown in importance in the West Wales economy employing over 50 trained local people. Such was their success that Rachel and Gareth were called on to give advice and information on organic food production to all sectors of the community. Suddenly everyone seemed interested.

But in essence, despite all the expansions and success, the company had remained at heart like the farm, a family business. Their children, Mark at Brynllys, John at the processing plant and Shan, the youngest, gaining experience helping on the farm until she married Alun in 1989, a local farmer from a nearby Penrhyncoch and left to bring up her own family. Neither Mark nor John is today involved in the business and are following their own interests, achieving their own objectives. Rachel and Gareth hoped they would both have stayed but it was not to be.

Mark the eldest had worked on the farm for years after leaving school and as parents they both believed that he would take over. As he grew up and matured, he became skilful and hard working. Then in his late 20s he decided to return to education and study for an MBA at university. It was a major step to undertake and by remaining focused and diligent on his studies he graduated in one year, not two.

"We were very proud parents on graduation day," recalls Rachel. "Not least because Mark hadn't had any formal higher academic education, except the more practical agricultural course at Gelli Aur Farm Institute. He's got really good skills. He articulates his thoughts well and I would say he's a people person," is his mother's observation.

John the second son was different. Whereas Mark had been an easy child, according to Rachel, "John was a shocker. The middle child of the three, he was the most challenging."

But John had a real talent which became apparent at an early age, namely, he had a great insight and understanding of horses. He was a gifted rider, competing and winning at shows all over the country including the Horse of the Year Show at Wembley. When he outgrew one pony and needed another, he and Gareth would look at advertisements in papers and magazines, read *Horse and Hound*, and then visit farms and stables during weekends. John was to reject many horses after riding and putting them through their paces but once he recognised a horse with talent, he knew his mind immediately. In true Welsh fashion, Gareth would haggle over the price, and once or twice they would return to Brynllys to think about a deal, only to find that by Monday the horse would have been sold to another buyer. Gareth soon realised that when it came to buying horses, John had a real gift for spotting an animal's potential and personality, so soon, whenever John said the words, 'that's the one', they bought immediately.

As a teenager, he became a successful horse rider and show jumper. They bought a thoroughbred gelding named 'Percy Special' and horse trials up and down the land brought the pair success. He was also selected to compete for a place in the British Junior Team. But unfortunately, Percy became lame with the result that the vet advised that he should be put down, an experience that at the time, caused severe distress and disappointment, so much so that John ceased riding altogether. As a young and developing partnership they were on the brink of great success and the trauma of those events remained with John for many years.

Keeping horses is of course a labour of love and to get to the top at equine events there is the grooming, cleaning bridles and saddles, feeding and mucking out and as a teenager John was not too keen on these aspects of preparation and presentation. He found his mother a willing helper but eventually it became a source of frustration and discord. After Percy, John left the farm to find work elsewhere and live with a friend in town, a kind of gap year, but when the dairy business began to grow and they needed a driver, John returned to take on that role plus marketing and sales and from then on Rachel recalls, "He committed himself. He stayed with us through thick and thin. He worked hard at all aspects of the company, became our General Manager and when we sold the company, John agreed to stay with the new management for two years."

John had dedicated himself to the company but when the two year agreement came to an end he gave the company six months notice that he wanted to leave. The very same day he became ill with a dramatic facial palsy and inflamed glands. His recovery was slow and painful and the company tried to persuade him to stay, but John wanted to move on. He had a dream and desire to travel, to have new experiences and when he was fully fit, he set off for Australia.

When he arrived in Australia, John decided to look up old friends, Ursula and Jim Lees, two people who had played an important part in his early life. Previously Jim had established an equine centre at Aberystwyth University and Ursula owned a riding school. She had spotted that John had a real talent worth nurturing and helped him to become established as a rider of ability. Subsequently, Ursula and Jim had moved to Australia to establish another riding centre.

"When John got there, he sat on a horse, the first time he had done so since Percy had been put down. There and then he decided, this is what I'm going to do, and that's what he's done. He's still out there, with his own thriving business. He's done it on his own and it's a success," Rachel explains with evident pride that the family's entrepreneurial spirit has been passed to the fourth generation.

Thus the two sons determined to follow their own course, something that one way and another seemed a male family trait, occasionally to the point of obduracy. But what of their daughter Shan?

"There are aspects in Shan that are very like her father. She is determined and hard working. She's inherited his organisational skills and she has patience. You need patience in farming," says Rachel.

Shan and Alun farm 700 acres in north Ceredigion and live near Penrhyncoch, a village some four miles from Brynllys. They have three teenage sons, Owain, Llyr and John who have inherited the work ethic and a love of rugby and football. In September 2007, Shan also gave birth to twins, a boy and a girl, Rachel Annie May and Thomas Ifan and the emphasis within the family changed. Before the twins, both parents had played an active part in community affairs. Shan had been chairman of the School Governors and Chair and President of the Aberystwyth Grassland Society. Surprisingly, she was also secretary of the local football club where she remains the Treasurer, an involvement that occasionally means not so much 'running the line,' but making others 'toe the line', using some straight-talking on the rules of good behaviour.

"They are both community orientated. Often Alun will sort out community problems before dealing with his own. If someone's in trouble, he's the first to help. That's the way he is and that's the way they are. It gives them satisfaction and pleasure," says Rachel. "It's a funny thing, I remember when Shan was born, I'd had two boys and the instant I was told it was a baby girl, I felt euphoria that the household would be much more balanced. It would still be three to two but now there would be another female. I've often wondered why I felt like that."

Asked if she is a feminist, Rachel says, "It depends how you define it, but yes, I suppose you can say I am in my own way. I mean Gareth was known in the family as a bit of a chauvinist. I understood that because on the whole men feel threatened by women who appear strong, who know their own minds. With a family of mainly men, it's diplomacy in this household!"

"I remember a story about Welsh Mam-gu in Llanwenog. She was also a strong woman. But women are strong in different ways. There's a story told that her husband, Thomas, announced one day that he wanted to leave their farm to open a hat shop in Lampeter. But she told him, you go, I'm staying on the farm! So you see, she didn't have legal rights but she spoke her mind, stood firm, unbowed and fearless!"

Joining the discussion, Rachel's mother Dinah says, "Men couldn't cope on their own you see. I think I'm like my Welsh Mamgu too. Men never worried mother and they've never worried me."

And Rachel adds, "Mum always treated men with respect, as an equal. She knew they had their way of doing things, she respected that, so they never felt threatened. As farmers, men can lead quite a solitary existence for much of the day. They appreciate the support of women in the home. There is therefore great respect for a widow who carries on farming alone after her husband has died."

Like her father Rachel describes herself as a peacemaker. "There's no point being confrontational. I try to present the alternative, although it may take longer and I may become frustrated, incredibly so sometimes, but I try always to find a resolution. Once you become confrontational, you lose your perspective."

Asked whether having a developing business partnership within a marriage was difficult, Rachel says, "No, but you have to work at it. Gareth is a very strong minded person. At times we may disagree but he and I always had the same goals. We cared for our children and we nurtured the land and our animals. We wanted the children to be secure. We were and are protective of them and we wanted the next generation to have opportunities."

*   *   *   *   *   *

By the end of the 1990s there had been tremendous growth. Twice they had invested in major expansions to the plant, proof that consumer interest and demand for organic foods was increasing. When they discussed plans for the future, Rachel and Gareth could see ever more expansion was necessary. They had spent 15 years in the food processing business and they were tired. It had been hard graft and the two years after the first huge investment in the new processing plant were the most pressurised. Meanwhile, debts had mounted and they were not generating enough money from sales to begin repayments.

Gareth had dealt with finances and the burden of knowing that every time he needed to borrow more money, he risked the fate of Brynllys and the family home. An entrepreneur by nature, he appeared to wear his concerns lightly but privately he felt the strain.

"We had driven ourselves to expand because if it had failed, we would have lost the farm. By 1999, I was tired and ready to get out," says Rachel.

Those first two years had left indelible memories of risk, financial pressures, and uncertainty but as Rachel acknowledges, "Gareth carried a lot of the financial responsibility and in all fairness he kept the information of our financial predicament to himself. The all-powerful motivation was the thought that we might lose Brynllys. When you're hungry and motivated you focus, and we simply said, we wouldn't let it happen."

They had come to the decision to sell the business which for Gareth was surprisingly not difficult. As he explains, "I'm quite good at sorting things out in my head. Make a decision, be decisive, right or wrong or you don't move on. Mind if you've made a mistake, you have to move twice as fast!"

Their initial deliberations had been prompted by a surprise offer to buy the company from one of the largest UK food companies in the country. They rejected it but the offer certainly focused their thoughts. Another company too made an approach but when that too was rejected, the original company returned to make a second bid. This time Rachel and Gareth were receptive and following consultations with the company's acquisition manager, they formalised a 'heads up' agreement, a legally binding exchange of intent and information which is not divulged, even if there is a failure to reach a final sale.

Information flowed and negotiations progressed to the point that they reached a ballpark price. Within a few days, when Gareth had gone away to attend a three day conference, the acquisition manager phoned Brynllys to make an appointment. He then drove down to meet them but when Gareth arrived home for the meeting, he remembers Rachel greeted him with the words, "He's gone. I've pulled out of the deal."

Gareth explains, 'We had a good relationship with the acquisition manager, we got on well with him. He had come here to say that he felt his company were taking advantage of us. The fact was that the company was buying us out in order to take us out of the market. They were buying our product in order to finish it. The dairy in Aberystwyth would be closed. We just couldn't believe it. We were so proud that a big company like that wanted to develop Rachel's, we didn't see their real intention. We learnt a very big lesson at that point. Rachel told the representative there was no way we could consider any deal on that basis."

The commercial world of big business had shown its sharp teeth and although they had believed the company had the necessary funds and the intention to take the Rachel's brand and the company forward, it was not to be.

"Fortunately our instincts and drive had made us successful to a point. But I didn't feel we had all the skills necessary to take it much further," says Gareth. "The prospect of a sale seemed very timely but having raised the wind, we were back to square one."

The failure to negotiate a deal was a bitter disappointment but as things unfolded, the tip-off to withdraw and cancel further negotiations had come at the right moment. Within a few months another, very different company appeared on the horizon.

Horizon Organic Dairy is a leading organic American company based in Colorado. Founded in 1991 it is specifically focused on organic milk and dairy products. Horizon had been founded by a charismatic entrepreneur, Mark Retzloff who had expertise in the natural foods sector and a passion for organic farming. Together with his colleague Paul Repetto, Mark pioneered the search for organic milk supplies from family farms to make organic dairy products available in the US under the Horizon Organic brand. Today it remains the leading American brand of certified organic milk and related products.

The two entrepreneurs also bought farms, first in Idaho then Maryland, California and Colorado to pioneer organic dairy farming practices in different states. Like the Rowlands in Wales, theirs was a passion to explain and a mission to convince sceptics of the merits of natural food production.

From simple beginnings, Mark Retzloff's business acumen and that of the company saw such rapid growth that it led to the successful listing on the NASDAQ in 1996, with the sale of shares netting $46 million, including $24 million for acquisitions. Looking further afield, they were soon keen to develop the business internationally and had already outlined a strategy for Europe and Japan. With the wind in his sails and a fistful of dollars, Mark Retzloff set off to explore organic dairy opportunities abroad, which is what led him to the UK and eventually to Wales and Rachel's.

The story and development of Rachel's Dairy had many parallels with Horizon, not least a quality product, value in the brand, good production practices and staff relations. It was also led by two inspired entrepreneurs. When the principals met, in many ways it was a meeting of minds. Most importantly, Gareth and Rachel were inspired by Mark's enthusiastic approach.

Following detailed research into Horizon's aspirations, the veracity and accuracy of their investment and marketing plans, managerial structures and a wide range of other details, Rachel and Gareth were satisfied that Rachel's would benefit from an agreement with Horizon. The deal was completed and signed on 31st March 1999 but with certain guaranteed stipulations.

Horizon agreed to retain the name, Rachel's and to retain Rachel and Gareth as consultants and ambassadors for the company. They also agreed that the processing plant would remain in Aberystwyth at the heart of the organic milk producing area of Wales. When the plant first opened, it had been one of few major dairy processing plant in Wales. Within eight years Rachel's Dairy had become a leading brand, a Welsh icon, so for the Rowlands it was important that Horizon continued to underline its Welsh heritage in their marketing plans. Today all Rachel's yogurts still carry the bilingual slogan, *'Bwyd Da o Gymru – Good Food From Wales'*. As the organic movement continued to grow with supermarkets devoting ever more shelves to organic products, the Welsh identity was an important element of the Rachel's Dairy strategy to emphasise the background and provenance.

Meanwhile farmers in Britain had seen a number of agri-food disasters and food scares that had blighted their livelihoods. From the Chernobyl nuclear fall-out in 1986 affecting upland sheep farming in Wales, to salmonella in eggs, listeria in cheese (1988-9) and BSE (Bovine spongiform encephalitis) 1996-9 and Foot and Mouth in 2001. These devastating incidents had alerted the public to issues surrounding intensive farming and food production. As a result, sales of organics increased as consumers became more aware of the benefits of traditional methods of farm production and food they could trust.

In this respect, the Horizon deal brought another related local bonus. Aberystwyth was a university town with a strong agricultural department concentrating its teaching and research on conventional farming. Organic farming seemed to arouse considerable prejudice and scepticism within the academic fraternity. The dismissive attitude was understandable because it was research by scientists in the early days that had emphasised efficiency and greater productivity from chemicals and additional fertilisers. Horizon had found a similar attitude in the USA and this was the main reason why they bought farms to counter arguments by regularly researching and rigorously analysing organic milk production.

Research was invaluable and Horizon was similarly prepared to invest in UK research too. They offered a sum of £20,000 for five years to fund a post for the Department of Agriculture to concentrate specifically on organic dairy farming. The Vice-Chancellor, Dr Derec Llwyd Morgan welcomed the initiative and for Rachel and Gareth it was a dream come true, for they had longed to establish a centre for organic education and research at Aberystwyth. Today the Organic Centre of Wales is a great success. It acts as a focal point for the dissemination of information, education, policy and strategy and provides support for the entire organic community in Wales.

For the family at Brynllys, Horizon's sponsorship decision had a certain poignancy. It was exactly 100 years since Bessie Brown had travelled from Scotland to become a member of the University Agricultural Department!

*   *   *   *   *

It would be natural to assume that relinquishing the role of directly managing the company they owned, Rachel and Gareth would have time to relax. For close on 20 years theirs had been a pressured way of life with many risks to overcome. Selling the company was a tremendous relief but it was also tinged with not a little sadness. They were leaving staff, many of whom had been with them from the very early days as a farm dairy. Would a big company from another country and culture and with another set of working practices have the same ethos, or the same attitude to staff who had been like an extended family?

Rachel was pleased that the agreement had ensured they would both remain a part of the business as consultants. Ten years on she reflects, "I enjoy the fact that we're still involved. Much of the responsibility is somewhere else but I do get satisfaction knowing I can still make a contribution."

Horizon invested heavily in staff training to identify opportunities and weaknesses within the Aberystwyth processing plant. They were also very focused on marketing. It was a fast growing business. Consumer demand for organic products was expanding and required major investments for further mechanisation. Meanwhile promotion, sales and new product development would call for different skills. The technology was becoming complex and Horizon could see the need for personnel who possessed the relevant qualifications and understanding of highly technical procedures. The company began recruiting high-flyers.

When the sale of Rachel's Dairy agreement had been signed and sealed, Horizon had immediately announced that they planned to introduce branded organic milk as part of their UK strategic marketing plans. They could now offer retailers a full service of organic milk products and marketing support to ensure Rachel's yogurts would gain wider presence in shops and stores.

Initially Mark Retzloff had ambitions for Horizon as a potential world brand and he was fascinated by the fact that in Britain there was no branded milk. Milk was predominantly either sold effectively as a commodity item under a supermarket's own-brand or by doorstop delivery in anonymous bottles. He saw a clear opportunity but was first stumped by the limited supplies of organic milk in the UK, almost all of which were directly contracted to the major supermarkets.

A protracted period of negotiation and discussion with different parties eventually saw one supermarket acknowledge that, if they were to grow sales of organic milk much more, then possibly a branded milk could do the trick. But as things worked out it was not Horizon but the Rachel's brand that triumphed when extensive market research showed that the reputation and position of Rachel's via its yogurts was more attractive to consumers. And thus Rachel's notched up a further pioneering first as it became Britain's first branded milk!

Next, came detailed plans for further extensions to the processing plant providing extra office space and a refrigerated fruit and packing room. As Gareth said at the time, "The company was able to continue where we left off and in the way we wanted it to. They recruited 50 extra staff making the total work-force of over 100 local people in full employment. In two years the turn-over doubled, producing 10 million pots of yogurt a year."

A further investment of £3m was found to build a huge extension. The direct investment from the US of £1.9 million was matched by a substantial processing and marketing grant by the Welsh Assembly Government. Construction began in 2003 and when the opening ceremony took place in November 2004 by First Minister, Rhodri Morgan AM, the workforce was increasing to 140 and the daily output reached 50 tonnes of yogurt per day. The figures drip onto the page, litres of milk changing overnight to tonnes of yogurt.

Such an increase in output was also dependent on a constant supply of quality organic milk. When Rachel began in the 1982 snowstorm there were only five certified organic farms in Wales. By December 2006 there were more than 700 with 83 licensed organic milk producers and another 12 were in the process of converting to the organic system. This was in no small part due to the inspiration of Rachel's and the company's ability to process and add value to organic milk. The fact that organic milk producers were given a 10p-a-litre premium on the usual farm gate price was one of the major reasons why the rate of change to the organic system in Wales increased.

Other benefits to the agricultural community ensued. In 2000, 20 organic dairy farmers from all parts of Wales came together to form the cooperative Calon Wen. Their aim was to support organic food processing in Wales and to secure a long term market for organic milk produced by Welsh farmers. It was the first company in the UK to achieve the Soil Association Ethical

Trade Symbol and when they proved that they could provide high quality milk and give a consistent and frequent service, Rachel's offered a long term agreement.

Rachel's were also able to extend the range and nature of its products – plain yogurt, Greek, fat free and low fat, bio-live plus yogurt desserts and drinks; cream, crème fraiche and butter. The development of new products, the expansion of the processing plant, the engagement of a co-operative like Calon Wen and the constant review of the brand and marketing techniques has ensured that Rachel's remains central to the local economy of West Wales.

*   *   *   *

As the activity generated by Rachel's Dairy expanded, it would have been natural for Gareth and Rachel to settle into a more leisurely way of life but their sense of public service has propelled them into other activities within the farming world. Rachel had already been awarded with the MBE for her services to Welsh agriculture in the 1997 Queen's Honours List. As the new millennium dawned she could again concentrate on her first love, the farm and the pedigree herd of Guernsey cattle. The farm had remained a thriving enterprise during all the years of developing the Rachel's Dairy processing plant but now she could give it her full attention. Meanwhile Gareth was invited by the Welsh Assembly Government to become Chairman of the Agri-Food Partnership Welsh Organic Strategy Group with a remit to look into the future of organic farming.

As retirement loomed, they began reviewing plans for the future of Brynllys as an organic dairy farm and Rachel and Gareth were forced to re-consider their options. Farming was a heavy commitment and labour intensive. The work involved with the herd meant milking twice a day and the financial returns for the product, in addition to rising production, costs were a consideration. Finding staff was becoming more difficult, especially a herdsman who could take responsibility, who understood dairy cows and could manage them effectively and in line with organic methods.

"You need to have an understanding of what animals need. So many trained people are tied to using drugs, whereas we tend to manage without using them. It can be done," says Rachel.

The over-riding factor in all their deliberations was the fact that Brynllys was truly organic and had been so for 60 years and more. Their belief in the principles and systems remained as strong as ever. It was a heritage to be handed on to the next generation and Shan, the youngest of their three children had become the obvious choice. Her heart was in farming and she was totally committed to the organic system.

But Shan's commitment was taking its toll. Milking twice a day was an added tie and pressure in what was already a busy life. Rachel could see the dangers for Shan leaving her home six miles away and arriving every day at five in the morning for milking and managing the cows.

Rachel decided it was too much, "No, I said, this is doing you no good, not for you or the family if you have to run a dairy herd in addition to your other commitments."

It was time for another pragmatic decision. After much heart searching, they decided eventually to sell their pedigree herd of Guernsey cattle and turn to beef cattle and sheep. It was a wrench, especially for Rachel's mother, Dinah, who saw years of her pedigree breeding work about to disappear but she gave them her full backing. They sold all the cows, apart from two kept to provide milk for the extended family. The milking parlour too was sold and today, the old stone cowshed with the original stalls remains empty, as does the dairy with the milk separator and the tank storage area.

It was a sad day for Rachel and Gareth when the link between Rachel's processing plant ceased to receive Guernsey milk from Brynllys as the farm's focus changed from dairy to beef cattle. However they have now chosen to develop a pedigree herd of indigenous Welsh Black Cattle in addition to the Limousin, a specialised beef producing animal introduced to the UK from France in 1971 and recognised for its sturdiness, health and adaptability.

Rachel recalls, "It was difficult to see the farm without the Guernseys out in the fields. But instead we've now got Welsh Blacks. We've always known that they produce quality meat, so you see we've started again with another quality organic product."

Both breeds have become a source of huge interest and pleasure. "It's important to know where your stock comes from and be able to improve and follow certain lines and characteristics," says Rachel.

From the day Shan pledged to maintain the farm as organic, Rachel and Gareth could look to the future. There was excitement and pride in Gareth's voice when he remarked, "I'm looking forward to one of the grandchildren coming here, moving in and having responsibility. It would be nice if he or she would walk with us, very much as we did with Rachel's mother to get the experience, to pick up the principles of breeding. Shan has got the eye. You need knowledge and experience as well as the interest. The point with beef cattle is that you are not only developing breeding stock but also ultimately meat for the butcher and the consumer."

They had intended to develop a flock of Welsh Mountain sheep but finally, decided on Texels which they cross with Suffolk rams to produce top quality prime organic Welsh lamb. Texels originated on one of the Friesan islands, the Isle of Texel and are remarkable for their muscle development. The Suffolk is a breed that is considered the UK's flagship stock.

And there is one other breed of sheep which has become an all-consuming hobby for grandson Llyr. Five years ago he was given five ewes and a ram of one of the distinctive mountain breeds indigenous to Wales, the Torwen meaning 'white belly' in Welsh. They are small, attractive and personable, noted for their black/brown colour and distinctive white stomachs. They are hardy and known for their strong mothering features. Llyr now has a flock of 70 and they are his pride and joy so that when he and his grandfather enter into a serious discussion on breeding and husbandry, he can more than hold his own.

Walking the farm is a daily delight for Rachel and Gareth, observing and noting closely any small changes in livestock and grazing pastures. Dinah too at 97 still enjoys walking the fields, casting an experienced eye over everything and deriving great satisfaction from the experience and legacy she continues to pass on to future generations of the family. In their time as organic farmers, they have all experienced the derision of others, have been dismissed as cranks, described as 'muck and magic' farmers and being side-lined from meaningful agricultural discussion.

But now the world has come full circle. They have the satisfaction of knowing that by sticking to their principles, they have helped pioneer a quiet revolution in quality food and have succeeded in making organics fashionable and widely understood.

*   *   *   *   *   *

In the last few years, as well as remaining involved in the company, Gareth and Rachel have taken on a number of high profile public roles. In 2002 Rachel became the first True Taste of Wales Ambassador, an initiative created by the Welsh Assembly Government to promote and endorse the use of quality Welsh produce in the hospitality and tourism industry in Wales. There was a buzz of excitement and expectation the night of the announcement when 500 people sat down to dinner at the Celtic Manor Hotel and although Rachel knew the result in advance, she trembled as she walked to the stage.

"I felt very, very humble. I had tried to memorise my acceptance speech and somehow or other, I delivered it without looking at my notes. I know I didn't because they were still in my pocket!" she recalls.

It was a role that gave her a particular pleasure and gave her the ideal platform to promote the quality of Welsh food products at national and international level. She also travelled to Europe and New York to functions representing the agriculture and food industry in Wales. For Rachel, the main thrust of her ambassadorial year was to give both sides of the food industry in Wales, producers and consumers, greater confidence in the quality of Welsh products.

Many producers are still small family farmers who have diversified operations to increase their income by selling direct to the consumer. Others, like Tŷ Nant water, with the iconic blue bottle and Halen Môn, natural salt from the sea, have achieved international status through bold and creative branding and promotion. Whether they are large or small companies, there is the added bonus of creating employment in rural areas. Real progress has been achieved and as the first True Taste Ambassador, Rachel saw her main role as giving credibility to the industry delivering a message that Wales was producing and promoting quality products.

In 2000, both Rachel and Gareth were made Honorary Fellows of Aberystwyth University and Rachel in particular is much involved serving on numerous committees and the University Council.

More recently Gareth has undertaken a role working with local farmers to help them add value to their premium produce. He now chairs the food marketing group of the Cambrian Mountains Initiative, a project inspired and led by HRH The Prince of Wales. The initiative is designed to help sustain farming families in upland Wales. In 2009 Gareth also became High Sheriff of Dyfed.

Thus Rachel and Gareth are by no means retired but their day-to-day responsibilities have changed. No longer milking twice a day and no longer running a multi-million pound manufacturing business, nevertheless, their experience and knowledge is much in demand when future agricultural and environmental policies are being discussed.

Meanwhile, the future of Brynllys as an organic farm is secure with their daughter. Shan has taken on that responsibility and finally, with the birth of twins, a boy and a girl, the fifth generation of women is growing up.

* * * * * *

When Bessie Brown came to Aberystwyth from Scotland over a hundred years ago little did she realise she was to leave such a proud legacy of achievement on the land, albeit based on hard work, bravery and diligence, from humble beginnings and against all odds.

Her daughter Dinah took up the torch for organic farming, becoming a knowledgeable and forthright ambassador for the Soil Association, a pedigree livestock breeder and farmer of distinction.

Bessie's grand-daughter Rachel drew from that deep well of experience and knowledge and took the opportunity to prove that it was possible to establish a hugely successful business from local natural produce from quality from Welsh organic farms.

The combined accomplishments of the three generations span the panoramic history of agriculture in the 20th century, despite the fact that women were, in those decades, and maybe still are, under-represented in farming organisations and in agricultural politics.

All three have accomplished a great deal on their own terms. Above all, they dared to be different and defy convention.

"I hope my grandmother would approve" says Rachel. "She instilled in us all a fundamental belief in the power of nature and the importance of good husbandry to produce wholesome nutritious food. She never wavered from her beliefs, neither did Mother and nor did I. These are simply our family values."

*   *   *   *   *   *